Pro Salesforce Analytics Cloud

A Guide to Wave Platform, Builder, and Explorer

William Smith

Helen Sun

Apress®

ISBN-13 (pbk): 978-1-4842-1204-2

ISBN-13 (electronic): 978-1-4842-1203-5

Managing Director: Welmoed Spahr
Acquisitions Editor: Susan McDermott
Technical Reviewers: Mike Martin, Carl Brundage
Editorial Board: Steve Anglin, Pramila Balen, Louise Corrigan, James DeWolf, Jonathan Gennick, Robert Hutchinson, Celestin Suresh John, Michelle Lowman, James Markham, Susan McDermott, Matthew Moodie, Jeffrey Pepper, Douglas Pundick, Ben Renow-Clarke, Gwenan Spearing
Coordinating Editor: Rita Fernando
Copy Editor: Carole Berglie
Compositor: SPi Global
Indexer: SPi Global
Cover Designer: Friedhelm Steinen-Broo

Distributed to the book trade worldwide by Springer Science+Business Media New York, 233 Spring Street, 6th Floor, New York, NY 10013. Phone 1-800-SPRINGER, fax (201) 348-4505, e-mail orders-ny@springer-sbm.com, or visit www.springer.com. Apress Media, LLC is a California LLC and the sole member (owner) is Springer Science + Business Media Finance Inc (SSBM Finance Inc). SSBM Finance Inc is a Delaware corporation.

For information on translations, please e-mail rights@apress.com, or visit www.apress.com.

Apress and friends of ED books may be purchased in bulk for academic, corporate, or promotional use. eBook versions and licenses are also available for most titles. For more information, reference our Special Bulk Sales–eBook Licensing web page at www.apress.com/bulk-sales.

Any source code or other supplementary materials referenced by the author in this text is available to readers at www.apress.com. For detailed information about how to locate your book's source code, go to www.apress.com/source-code/.

For Nathaniel G. Smith

Contents at a Glance

About the Authors.. xiii

About the Technical Reviewers xv

Acknowledgments.. xvii

Introduction xix

▇Part I: A Complete Guide to the Salesforce Analytics Cloud 1

▇Chapter 1: An Overview of the Salesforce Analytics Cloud 3

▇Chapter 2: The Salesforce Analytics Cloud Explorer 15

▇Chapter 3: Analytics Cloud Builder.. 39

▇Chapter 4: Salesforce Analytics Platform... 77

▇Part II: Business Analytics Solutions Using the
Salesforce Analytics Cloud 87

▇Chapter 5: Critical Decision Making and the Salesforce Analytics Cloud 89

▇Chapter 6: Mobile Enterprise Data Discovery... 111

▇Chapter 7: Advanced Data Acquisition and Processing 141

Index.. 157

Contents

About the Authors.. xiii

About the Technical Reviewers xv

Acknowledgments.. xvii

Introduction xix

■Part I: A Complete Guide to the Salesforce Analytics Cloud 1

■Chapter 1: An Overview of the Salesforce Analytics Cloud 3

Evolution of Business Intelligence and Reporting Systems 3

The Challenge of Data Variety 5

    Data Uncertainty... 5

    The Scarcity of Personnel... 6

Data Discovery 7

    Self-Service Application Development and Analytic Interface... 8

    A Data Server... 8

    Data-Loading Interfaces and APIs 8

    An Alternative to the Data Lake 8

Introduction to the Salesforce Analytics Cloud... 9

    The Mobile Platform 9

    The Desktop Platform... 10

Advantages of the Salesforce Analytics Cloud 12

    The Cloud Architecture 12

    Mobile First 12

    Integration with the Salesforce Ecosystem 12

Conclusion... 13

■Chapter 2: The Salesforce Analytics Cloud Explorer 15

What Is Cloud Explorer? 15

The Two Versions of the Salesforce Analytics Cloud 15

Getting Started with Cloud Explorer 16

Launching Cloud Explorer 16

Datasets 19

Row-Level Security for Datasets 19

Lenses 19

Measures 19

Dimensions 20

Dates 22

Bringing It All Together 23

Learn by Doing 26

Lens Modification History, Undo, and Replay 27

Exploring the Data 27

Mobile Lens Creation 28

Dashboards 28

Widgets 28

Data Display Widgets 29

Selector Widgets 30

Display Widgets 31

The Dashboard Development Cycle 32

Link Back to Lens 34

Dashboard Wrap-Up 36

Apps 36

My Private App 36

The Share Button 36

Playground Data 37

What Wave Lacks 37

    Text Processing and Analysis 38

    Map and Geospatial Data.. 38

    Advanced Math and Statistical Functions 38

Conclusion... 38

■Chapter 3: Analytics Cloud Builder.. 39

Building a Simple Dashboard.. 39

    Loading Dataset.. 39

    Creating a Dashboard... 44

Dashboard Design Aesthetics.. 54

    Steps to Design Aesthetic Dashboards.. 55

Mobile Dashboard Designer 56

    Upload Dataset Through Mobile Device.. 56

    Create Dashboard Using Mobile Designer 64

Advanced Dashboards... 70

    Anatomy of a dashboard.. 70

    Advanced Dashboard with SAQL 71

Summary.. 75

■Chapter 4: Salesforce Analytics Platform.. 77

Methods of Data Integration.. 77

External Data API... 79

    Step 1. Create .CSV File... 80

    Step 2. Create JSON Metadata 81

    Step 3. Upload Files.. 81

    Step 4. System Job Is Created and Run 81

    Step 5. Dataset Is Created 81

    Restrictions on Use... 81

    Supporting Documents.. 82

Extract Transform Load Tools 82

    Step 1. Connect to Source 83

    Step 2. Extract Data 84

    Step 3. Sort, Filter, and Transform 84

    Step 4. Determine the Dataset 84

    Step 5. Write the Dataset 84

Wave REST API 85

Conclusion 85

▉Part II: Business Analytics Solutions Using the
Salesforce Analytics Cloud 87

▉Chapter 5: Critical Decision Making and the Salesforce Analytics Cloud 89

Critical Decision Making and Cognitive Bias 89

The Use Case Manufacturer 90

    Early Glass Making 91

    Early Instrumentation and Increased Statistical Process Control 92

    Automatic Control via Computer Technology 92

    Data Networks Offer Increased Integration 92

Company Structure and Facilities 94

    Float Glass Plants 94

    Glass Fabrication Plants 94

    Automotive Encapsulation Facilities 94

    The Organization of the Company's Plants 95

Key Performance Indicators 96

Facility-Level Reporting 96

    Diagnosis of Machine Problem 100

    Eliminating Cognitive Bias with Data 103

Corporate-Level Reporting 104

    Assessing Plant Manager Performance 106

Conclusion 110

▓**Chapter 6: Mobile Enterprise Data Discovery**..**111**

Overview of Our Use Case.. 111

    The Traditional Approach to Reporting... 112

    An Alternative to the Traditional Approach.. 112

The Use Case Architecture 114

    Step 1 – Output to .CSV File 115

    Step 2 – User Access of .CSV File on Dropbox 116

    Step 3 – Modifying the Metadata and Creating the Dataset............................ 119

    Step 4 – Creating Lenses and Dashboards.. 122

Data Used in Our Use Case.. 122

    Sales Amount Data 123

    Date Data... 123

    Product Data.. 123

    Reseller Data 123

Dashboard Development Cycle 124

    Digging Deeper... 128

    Adding Other Dimensions: Evaluating Individual Contributors 136

    Analyzing Other Dimensions: Resellers 138

Security and Shared Public File Services.. 139

Conclusion.. 140

▓**Chapter 7: Advanced Data Acquisition and Processing** **141**

Data Acquisition—Tools and Technologies 141

    Web Scrapers 141

    Web Crawlers 142

    Text Analytics Processors 142

    Applications of These Tools 142

Data Processing—Terms and Concepts 145

Data Wrangling 145

Data Standards 145

Data Quality 145

Data Cleansing 146

Python: A Programming Language for Data Processing 146

Two Examples Using Python 148

Data Cleansing Example 1 148

Data Cleansing Example 2 150

Python Resources 154

Conclusion 155

Index 157

About the Authors

William Smith is Chief Architect at Vendita Technology Group, and where he is in charge of the Advanced Product Group. William is patented inventor of engineered systems for database and analytic systems, based on a converged infrastructure featuring both RISC and X86 processors. He is co-author of *Master Competitive Analytics with Oracle Endeca Information Discovery* (McGraw-Hill/Oracle Press) and has more than two decades experience as an enterprise architect with strong background in decision support systems and analytics. William's early career experience includes working with data from manufacturing control systems and instrumentation in industries that include plastics, petro-chemicals, glass, food, and extrusion processes. William has enterprise systems experience in higher education, finance, consumer research, and healthcare. His strong database administration and programming skills have enabled him to address analytical systems with a comprehensive and complete set of technical knowledge, resulting in top down designed systems and architectures. In the area of analytics, William began with working in the area of predictive failures and statistical process control. Later projects included utilization of advanced analytics technologies to provide insight in consumer research, institutional research, clinical informatics, and finance. William is currently working with customers making use of Big Data and is developing innovative solutions utilizing Salesforce Analytics Cloud.

Helen Sun, PhD, is the Vice President of Enterprise Architecture and Cloud Computing at Motorola Solutions with over 16 years of business and technology leadership experience in various industries including financial services, retail, CPG, logistics, healthcare, telecommunications, and utilities and with deep experience and proven expertise in analytics solutions and enterprise architecture. She is the co-author of *Oracle Big Data Handbook and Master Competitive Analytics with Oracle Endeca Information Discovery* (McGraw-Hill/Oracle Press). Helen is considered one of the Big Data luminaries in the industry.

About the Technical Reviewers

Mike Martin is a Solution Architect at Appirio where he is focused on helping Salesforce customers get the most out of their investment in the platform by scoping implementations and designing custom solutions for customers. Mike has completed the Salesforce Wave Analytics Cloud Brown Belt Accreditation and is a Certified Salesforce Administrator, Advanced Administrator, Sales Cloud Consultant, Service Cloud Consultant, Force.com Developer, and Platform App Builder. Mike has also been recognized as a Salesforce Community MVP and helps to lead the Indianapolis Salesforce User Group. He has been active in the Salesforce community since 2008.

Mike is a graduate of Rose-Hulman Institute of Technology with a BS in Computer Engineering and a Masters of Engineering Management. Mike currently lives in Indianapolis, IN with his wife, Jennifer, and two sons, Alexander and Jameson. When not working with Salesforce, you can probably find Mike enjoying a craft beer or helping with media and tech production at church. You can find Mike on Twitter: @ mikemartin_c.

Carl Brundage is passionate about data, analytics and software's ability to solve business challenges. Throughout his career, he has been a creator, whether it be technologies, departments, practices, products or customer success. Carl excels at the intersection of business and technology, where there is a need to create something new. He has delivered multiple presentations and blog posts on the Salesforce Analytics Cloud and earned Brown Belt Accreditation as an early adopter.

Recently, as a chief product evangelist, Carl does everything required to launch new products to the Salesforce App Exchange. From creating product roadmaps and developing marketing strategies to writing implementation guides and delivering demos, there is no job too big or small to tackle. In addition, he is a Salesforce certified Sales Cloud Consultant, Service Cloud Consultant, Pardot Consultant, Force.com Developer, Platform App Builder, Administrator, Advanced Administrator and Marketing Cloud Email Specialist. Connect with Carl on LinkedIn (https://www.linkedin.com/in/cbrundage) or follow him on Twitter (@carlbrundage).

Acknowledgments

We wish to gratefully acknowledge the assistance of our friend and colleague Paul Carlstoem in introducing us to the professionals at Apress. We would like to extend our gratitude to Susan McDermott and Rita Fernando at Apress for working so diligently on this title. Working with the team at Apress has been a pleasure and without their assistance, this book would not have been possible. We wish to extend our thanks to our technical editors, Mike Martin and Carl Brundage. We would like to acknowledge the assistance of Ciolek Ltd, Attorneys at Law in legal matters associated with our efforts as authors. Last, but not least, we wish to acknowledge the support of family and friends in their support our efforts as authors, especially our longtime friend and mentor Dr. Mesbeh Ahmed.

Introduction

Data discovery products are a category of analytics and business intelligence software that dominates new investment and has been gaining popularity, as organizations strive to enable decision-making with data. The reason for this popularity is not hard to understand. With data discovery software, everyday users can create applications that empower them as never before. Users are no longer dependent on their IT departments for reporting and data analysis needs. Data discovery users become "citizen data scientists," performing basic data analysis and finding correlations. This was previously possible only with high-end statistical analysis packages.

The Salesforce Analytics Cloud is a data discovery product introduced at the Salesforce conference Dreamforce in 2014, and has features that make it a compelling offering for organizations considering an investment in this exciting area of technology. It is 100% cloud-based, and adheres to Salesforce's strategy of "mobile first," with a fully functional mobile platform for creating and using data discovery applications. The pricing model for Salesforce Analytics Cloud allows organizations to adopt it with no capital investment. The Analytics Cloud is flat-fee subscription based, and is not subject to data transfer costs. Although the Salesforce Analytics Cloud is oriented towards everyday users, it also has advanced features that enable sophisticated applications to be developed by programmers. Support is available on a 24/7 basis and is included in some of the subscription packages.

Salesforce Analytics Cloud has built-in integration capabilities for building Salesforce Analytics Cloud applications with Salesforce data. It also has the capability of creating applications with data originating outside of Salesforce. This capability—creating applications with outside data—is the focus of this title.

Part 1 of this title provides guidance on using the Salesforce Analytics Cloud, introducing basic concepts, followed by more sophisticated usage.

Part II focuses on two use cases. The first use case features data from a corporation engaged in manufacturing. It has data from a wide variety of venues, from the factory floor to the executive suite. The second use case chapter illustrates how Salesforce Analytics Cloud is used with sales performance data, and is entirely developed on the Salesforce Analytics Cloud mobile interface. The final chapter covers advanced data acquisition and data processing, and covers how web scrapers and crawlers can be used to harvest data for use in Salesforce Analytics Cloud. This is followed by an overview of data processing, with a discussion on the Python programming language and how it can be used for data processing.

PART I

A Complete Guide to the Salesforce Analytics Cloud

CHAPTER 1

■ ■ ■

An Overview of the Salesforce Analytics Cloud

Know where to find information and how to use it; that is the secret of success.

—Albert Einstein

Einstein's sentiment, expressed in this concise quotation, captures our innate need to acquire and comprehend information. This is because information enables us to make decisions that are not impaired by bias or poor judgment. One could argue that this thought gave rise to computers, which were first developed to perform mathematical calculations faster. As computers have evolved, innovative strategies and technologies have also evolved to allow information in those computers to be more readily used in decision making. These strategies range from statistical methods to technologies that facilitate the storage of data for rapid retrieval, as well as visualization technologies.

In this book, we cover the Salesforce Analytics Cloud, one of the latest technologies to enable the productive use of information. The Salesforce Analytics Cloud belongs to a class of products known as "data discovery" products; this is the term that is usually used by research firms dealing with this technology. The Salesforce Analytics Cloud features a high-performance storage infrastructure that facilitates rapid data retrieval and advanced visualizations allowing information to be quickly understood, all delivered from the cloud infrastructure that underpins the success of Salesforce products. Before we delve into the Salesforce Analytics Cloud, though, let's set the context for this product and survey the data discovery products with a discussion of computers and technology in reporting and analytics.

Evolution of Business Intelligence and Reporting Systems

As computers evolved into systems to manage information, they were increasingly utilized in business and commerce. These early computers stored data in simple flat files. With increasing volumes of data, a more efficient and organized means of storing the data became necessary, which led to the creation of relational databases. Relational databases were capable of storing transactional data efficiently, but not in a manner that is easily queried or mined. The need to analyze information in transactional databases easily and quickly for reporting and analysis summoned into existence data warehouses and business intelligence (BI) tools. For over 20 years, these warehouses and tools have delivered reliable answers to typical questions, and they will continue to be used for the foreseeable future.

During this time, computer technology progressed at an astonishing rate, owing to increases in the power of microprocessors, the central "brain" of all computers. The 1980s marked the beginning of personal computer usage in business, with the introduction of the IBM personal computer in 1981, utilizing an Intel 8088 microprocessor with a total of 29,000 transistors (transistors are the electronic switches used in microprocessors). By the end of the 1980s, Intel Corporation had introduced the 80486, its first microprocessor having more than 1 million transistors. By 2014, the transistor count in Intel microprocessors exceeded 5.5 billion. Figure 1-1 illustrates the incredible rate of increase in transistor use since the first personal computer.

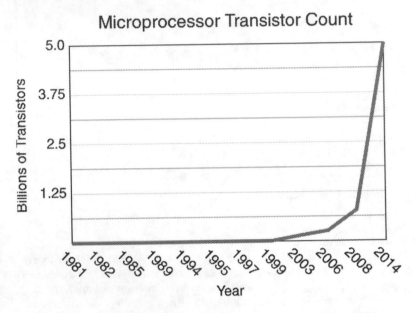

Figure 1-1. *Transistor count of Intel microprocessors from 1981 to 2014*

Intel has shipped over 200 million microprocessors whose collective transistor count is over 50 quadrillion, or put another way, more than 7 million CPU transistors for every person on earth. Microprocessors have long since left the confines of the personal computer, however, and have invaded nearly every aspect of our lives—in personal devices like smartphones and wearable health-monitoring devices, automotive control features, and "smart" meters monitoring the electric usage of our homes. It comes as no surprise, then, that this staggering amount of computing power produces an equally staggering amount of data.

Computer networking on a global scale has led to information sharing on an unprecedented scale, primarily through the Internet. The Internet has enabled communication media that command considerable attention in our daily lives: email, social media, and informative or sales websites. One commonality of all of this data is that it lies outside the transactional databases we mentioned earlier, and it is not easily accessible to BI tools for reporting and analysis. The growth of this data in the last decade has meant that 80 to 90 percent of the data relevant to individuals and organizations lies outside the transactional databases—and to a large extent, out of our reach.

Most of this data is classified as unstructured or semi-structured data because it lacks the strongly defined data types and well-defined data models found in structured data sources, like relational databases. Unstructured and semi-structured data does not have the static fields or organizational features of structured data sources. Table 1-1 lists examples of data sources that fall into each classification.

Table 1-1. *Data Types, Characteristics, and Examples*

Data Type	Characteristics	Example(s)
Structured data	Data model that has defined rectangular tables containing rows and columns, and referential integrity between tables	Relational databases (RDBMS)
Semi-structured data	Loosely defined data model, internal structure	XML, CSV, spreadsheet files (Excel), JSON
Unstructured data	No data model	Documents, email, social media, blogs, customer reviews, media files including image files and video

The Challenge of Data Variety

This unstructured and semi-structured data from many disparate sources has created a data management problem because the quantity of data and rate at which it is produced are beyond the processing capabilities of relational databases. Data having these attributes is known as "Big Data," and the most important attributes of Big Data are commonly referred to as "the three Vs," meaning the unusually high *volume* of the data, the *velocity* at which the data is produced, and the wide *variety* of sources of this data. To meet the challenges presented by Big Data, there has been strong interest in a class of clustered file-system technologies designed to store Big Data. By far the best known of these technologies is the Hadoop Distributed File System or HDFS, which is available through the Apache Foundation as Apache Hadoop; it is capable of coping with the volume and velocity problem of Big Data.

HDFS can be deployed on low-cost hardware, and the low upfront cost has created an incentive for HDFS to be used to aggregate all data—not just Big Data but also data originating in transactional systems like ERP and CRM systems, and even data from data warehouses. These large collections of data are sometimes referred to as "data lakes," since the data is simply "thrown" into them to be used later.

This brings us to the present-day challenge facing organizations that have created data lakes: it is difficult to get analytic value from data lakes at a speed that meets the needs and expectations of stakeholders and customers. There are two barriers impeding organizations from getting value from their Big Data investments.

Data Uncertainty

Figure 1-2 illustrates the progression to data lakes. The first barrier to getting value from Big Data is *data uncertainty*, and it derives from the "variety" aspect of the data. In the early days of HDFS, around 2010, there was a tendency to focus on the volume and velocity characteristics of Big Data, since the primary challenge was simply to store large amounts of rapidly produced data. The variety of data has proved to be full of problems and is the cause of data uncertainty. Most organizations are accustomed to the paradigm associated with data warehouses, for which typically there have been a small number of high-value data sources. These data sources are well understood and often well documented. By contrast, most data lakes have data from hundreds of data sources.

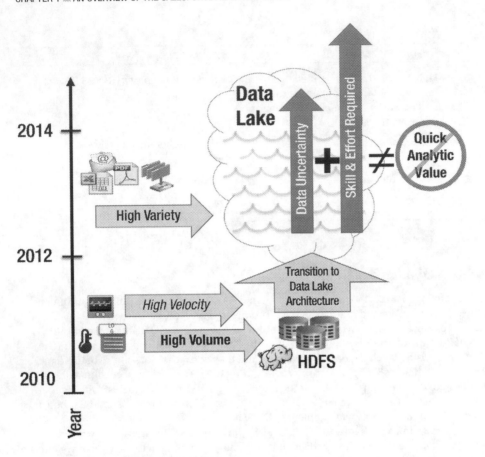

Figure 1-2. *The evolution of data lakes*

From the perspective of data analysts or users, there is a high degree of uncertainty as to what data is available and what the value is of the data that is being aggregated. With traditional BI and data warehouse solutions, 80 percent of the time needed to develop solutions to this uncertainty involves upfront tasks (e.g., requirements gathering, data modeling, data cleansing, and building the data warehouse). When we take into consideration the hundreds of data sources that would be represented in a data lake, much of them producing unstructured data, this time requirement only promises to increase. The impact of the large number of data sources, multiplied by the time involved for upfront tasks, makes data uncertainty a chronic problem.

The Scarcity of Personnel

The second barrier to getting value from Big Data involves a shortage of professionals who can work with these data sources. Data scientists and programmers who are skilled in working with Big Data are in short supply. The complexity of tools and programming knowledge required to extract information from HDFS are considerable, and as a result there are initiatives to access Big Data by using less complex tools like SQL. However, this approach has been largely ineffective at making Big Data more accessible, or at addressing the challenge of data uncertainty. This personnel problem is not easily addressed, as we cannot expect the supply of data scientists or programmers to increase anytime soon. In view of these two barriers, a better strategy is to rethink the current approach to Big Data and reconsider how we can work with unstructured data.

Data Discovery

To get past the need for data scientists and developers, an obvious solution is to provide interfaces that allow users to overcome the barrier of data uncertainty. Business analysts, data analysts, and subject-matter experts are accustomed to working with tools, and not command-line interfaces or code editors, so the interfaces must be of a graphic and intuitive nature.

The overall goal of these tools is to enable users to perform some of the basic tasks that would be performed by data scientists. Looking at the data-source record count, examining the distribution of the data versus time or other dimensions, and determining to the overall quality of the data are all basic tasks that can be performed with data discovery tools. With the capabilities of these data discovery tools, the data is "democratized" and users can become "citizen data scientists."

To understand how this is possible, let's examine some of the most prominent features of data discovery tools, focusing on the Salesforce Analytics Cloud. Figure 1-3 shows a simple logical diagram of a data discovery platform.

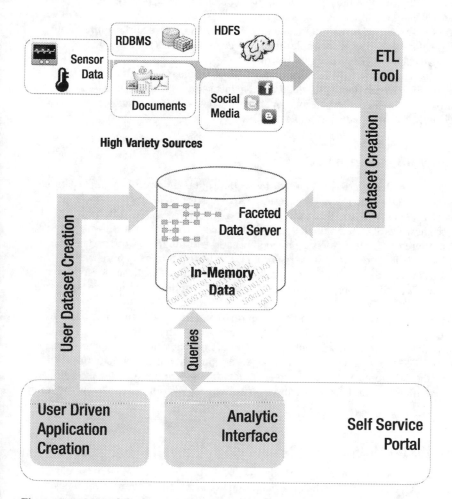

Figure 1-3. Logical diagram of data discovery platform

Self-Service Application Development and Analytic Interface

The Salesforce Analytics Cloud features a self-service portal that allows users to provision their own datasets and then to create analytic applications that use those datasets. For more complex data sources, programmers can create datasets and make them available to the portal users.

The analytic capability of the Salesforce Analytics Cloud relies on its visualization tools to give users the ability to easily understand data; they can also apply refinements by clicking on part of visualization and observing the changes that occur in other visualizations or table components. In this way, the Salesforce Analytics Cloud is capable of performing descriptive analytics, answering the question "What happened?"; it excels at diagnostic analytics, also answering the question "Why did it happen?"

A Data Server

The Salesforce Analytics Cloud features a data server that is specially designed to facilitate analytics and data discovery. This data server should not be confused with relational database servers; it has a much different way of storing data and establishing relationships between data.

The design of this data server is based on a faceted data model, whereby each record captured from a source is stored as an independent record, and each column in the record becomes an attribute, or "facet," of the record. Indexes are built on each facet, allowing rapid retrieval.

The Salesforce Analytics Cloud allows real-time exploration of data, which involves navigating all the records in a dataset in real time. When data is queried from the data server during such real-time exploration, the records are held in memory. This in-memory aspect of data discovery data servers is critical for achieving performance in real-time data exploration.

Data-Loading Interfaces and APIs

The Salesforce Analytics Cloud provides a variety of methods for loading data. End users can create datasets and load data into them from a web user interface. The Salesforce Analytics Cloud also provides web services to load the data. Specifically, the Salesforce Analytics Cloud supports both the venerable XML-based Simple Object Access Protocol, also known as SOAP, and the Representational State Transfer, also known as REST.

Support for Extract Transfer Load, or ETL, tools is provided primarily through the web services to load data into the Wave data server. Many other data discovery products require customers to purchase and use ETL tools that have been developed specifically for their data discovery products. Because Salesforce fosters partnerships with other IT product companies, a wide range of ETL products support the Salesforce Analytics Cloud.

The Salesforce Analytics Cloud is a complete technical solution for capturing and storing data, as well as deriving analytic value from it. The Salesforce Analytics Cloud is agnostic to the variety of source data, and is adept at processing both structured data and unstructured data. Compare this to the technologies associated with Big Data like HDFS, which only provide a storage solution, and it is not difficult to see why data discovery products like the Salesforce Analytics Cloud are enjoying a high adoption rate. According to Gartner Inc., the leading technology research firm, data discovery products now dominate all new spending on BI and analytic tools.

An Alternative to the Data Lake

For organizations working to find a strategy for managing the 80 to 90 percent of their data that is semi-structured or unstructured, which can co-exist with data originating from structured sources, the Salesforce Analytics Cloud is an alternative. No data discovery solution has the capacity of HDFS, so is not appropriate for the capture of massive volumes of data. However, for data that is unstructured, that does not have high volume or velocity, the Salesforce Analytics Cloud can be an alternative to dumping the data into a data lake.

The advantage of this scenario is that many data sources can be loaded into the Salesforce Analytics Cloud datasets with little or no involvement from IT personnel. With the Salesforce Analytics Cloud, users can create applications to provide graphics and tabular viewing tools that have short development cycles, often only a few hours.

The Salesforce Analytics Cloud can also be used to develop dashboards and quick reports against sources that are entirely transactional. With data discovery tools, it is far easier to "go the last mile" than with traditional BI and reporting tools. Users have less inclination to create "rogue" business processes by running ad hoc queries into office tools like Microsoft Excel to perform analysis, and will instead use the Salesforce Analytics Cloud.

Introduction to the Salesforce Analytics Cloud

Let's take a closer look at the Salesforce Analytics Cloud and see its two major platforms: mobile and desktop. Keep in mind that this information is merely an overview of features that are covered in more detail in Chapters 2, 3, and 4.

The Mobile Platform

The Salesforce Analytics Cloud provides "analytics to go," with its mobile-first emphasis. Now, analytics are no farther away than your back pocket. During the heady days of the Apple iPhone release in 2007, Steve Jobs stressed that the iPhone was something you would slip into the back pocket of your blue jeans, a mobile computing platform always available, no farther away than your wallet or keys.

Since the release of the iPhone, mobile access has been one of the most compelling applications of cloud computing, using its touch display to provide a rich interface connecting to a cloud-based infrastructure—yet one that remains hidden from the user. Smartphones and their direct descendants, tablet computers, have been primarily used for consuming data, mostly owing to the difficulty of creating content on a small screen and an onscreen keyboard. However, as users have begun considering these devices as the primary interface in their digital lives, software designers have responded by providing mobile applications that have sophisticated capabilities for creating content. The Salesforce Analytics Cloud follows this trend, allowing users to upload data, create views on the data, then incorporate those views into dashboards.

With the Salesforce Analytics Cloud mobile app, users can provision datasets from comma-separated value (.csv) files, tab separated-value files (TSV), Microsoft Excel files, and zip files containing these file types. The files are accessed from a mobile device, including files from websites, email attachments, and file repository services like Dropbox and Salesforce files. Once a dataset is created, users can create "lenses," which are views of the data using filters and sortation. The lenses have either a graphic or a tabular component, viewable on the mobile device. Dashboards can be accessed and created on mobile devices as well; they are collections of lenses that provide multiple or combined views of the data. Users can share their findings with others by taking screenshots of graphic elements or sending the .csv extracts from tabular components.

In April 2015, Apple released the Apple Watch, a device that Apple calls its "most personal device ever." The Salesforce Analytics Cloud has an application for the Apple Watch that provides access to dashboards or lens, allowing users to navigate their data using the watch's touch screen interface and digital crown.

Figure 1-4 shows the major components of the Salesforce Analytics Cloud for the mobile analytics experience.

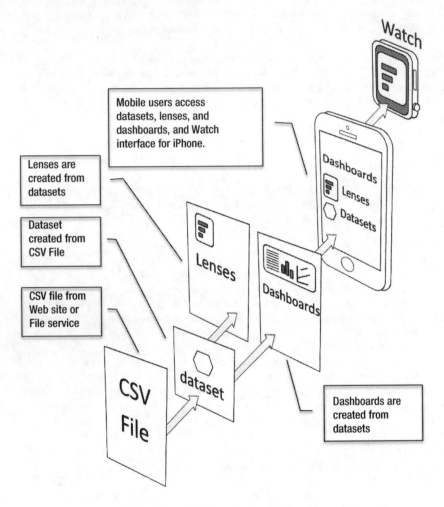

Figure 1-4. *Components of the Salesforce Analytics Cloud for mobile use*

The Desktop Platform

Figure 1-5 shows the components of the Salesforce Analytics Cloud desktop capabilities.

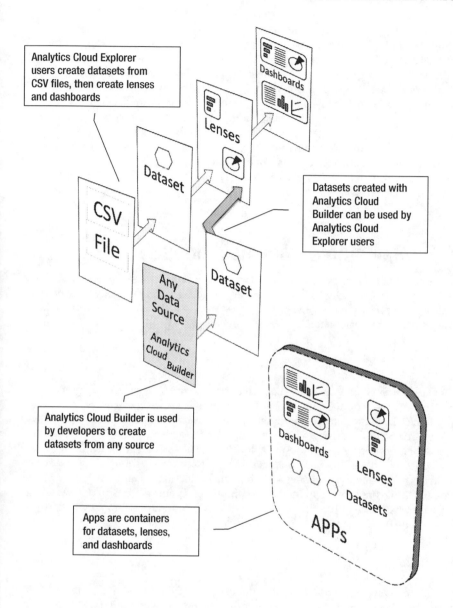

Figure 1-5. *Components of the Salesforce Analytics Cloud for desktop use*

The Salesforce Analytics Cloud desktop interface is the Analytics Cloud Explorer that allows users to create and use data discovery applications and dashboards. It can be accessed from a web browser, and it provides all the capabilities available from mobile interfaces, as well as additional features with regard to organizational and development capabilities. The Analytics Cloud Explorer has the same capabilities as described for the mobile app, but also the ability to create datasets from Salesforce objects. Once the datasets are created, they can be explored, allowing users to drill into and filter the data. During this exploration of data, users can create lenses, and these lenses can be used on the mobile app as well.

Additional functionality of the Analytics Cloud Explorer includes creating dashboards from lenses using an editor with graphic and tabular elements, along with widgets for creating text boxes, other graphic elements, and hyperlinks. Inside the dashboards, when a user drills into a dataset on one component, all the other components in the dashboard are updated. Put another way, if a user refines any data, all the other components in the dashboard are changed to reflect this refinement. This powerful feature allows coordinated exploration of data with all controls in a dashboard, as well as facilitating data discovery.

The highest level of abstraction in the Analytics Cloud Explorer is its apps, which can include many dashboards, lenses, and datasets. The apps can be thought of as containers for all of those objects, serving primarily as a grouping or bundling mechanism. Within the apps can be dashboards, lenses, and datasets. The contents of an app are left to the discretion of the users. For example, a user developing data discovery analytics around meteorological data might include a dataset from NOAA, along with dashboards and lenses within the app, but could also include datasets with data from an academic source or data collected by meteorological agencies outside the United States.

Advantages of the Salesforce Analytics Cloud

Now Data discovery products are not new to the world of analytics and business intelligence, of course, and when the Salesforce Analytics Cloud was introduced in 2014, into an already crowded market, this may have been viewed as a disadvantage. However, by coming in later the Salesforce Analytics Cloud has avoided the pitfalls and limitations experienced with earlier data discovery products.

The Cloud Architecture

The Salesforce Analytics Cloud has some unique features that set it apart from other data discovery products. For instance, since its introduction it has been 100 percent cloud based. Many other data discovery products have complex and elaborate infrastructures oriented toward "on-premise" installations; they must be installed and maintained by systems administrators. Similarly, patches and upgrades to add new features or fix bugs require a planned outage, and they must be thoroughly tested before installation on older production systems. If the data discovery system is mission critical, then a secondary system must be installed and maintained to provide high availability, and this can involve complex network components like load balancers.

The cloud-based Salesforce Analytics Cloud eliminates the complex on-premise infrastructure and with it, the added complexities of high availability. Patches and updates are continuously applied to the Salesforce Analytics Cloud, so you are always using the most up-to-date version.

Mobile First

A unique feature of the Salesforce Analytics Cloud is its mobile-first approach. The Salesforce Analytics Cloud was designed with mobile users in mind, using both smartphones and tablet computers. Mobile users can create datasets and applications entirely on these mobile devices. The Salesforce Analytics Cloud also makes graphics and data discovery available on the Apple Watch, and is currently the only data discovery product with this capability.

Integration with the Salesforce Ecosystem

Datasets can easily be constructed from Salesforce objects for organizations that use the Salesforce sales and service cloud—and these can be combined with any other data source. Users can share data discovery applications with other users in the Salesforce ecosystem, including Chatter, the Salesforce social-enterprise cloud. This medium allows rapid and seamless sharing of results and eliminates the need to take screenshots of graphics or make extracts to share results.

Salesforce has a wide network of technology firms in its partnership ecosystem. This ecosystem enables those organizations that have already invested in analytics tools and infrastructure to enhance their investments with the Salesforce Analytics Cloud. Contrast this situation with other data discovery vendors who require the use of proprietary ETL tools for their products.

Conclusion

In this introductory chapter we have defined and described data discovery, and showed why it is an attractive alternative to forming data lakes for certain types of data. We explored the general features of data discovery and then looked at how the Salesforce Analytics Cloud offers expanded discovery tools. We are now ready to examine the Salesforce Analytics Cloud in detail in the next three chapters. Those chapters will then be followed by others with industry-specific use cases that demonstrate how the Salesforce Analytics Cloud can be applied to deliver analytic value efficiently and effectively.

Here are the chapters in this book, grouped into two parts.

Part 1: A Complete Guide to the Salesforce Analytics Cloud

Part 1 comprises Chapters 1 through 4. Chapter 1 offers a brief overview and introduction. Chapter 2 covers the Analytics Cloud Explorer, while Chapter 3 provides an in-depth tutorial on the Analytics Cloud Builder, and covers the creation of datasets, lenses, dashboards, and apps. Chapter 4 is intended for developers who will be using integration tools to create analytical applications in the Salesforce Analytics Cloud Wave platform.

Part 2: Business Analytics Solutions Using the Salesforce Analytics Cloud

Part 2 comprises Chapters 5 through 7.Chapter 5 starts with a discussion on critical decision making and data discovery, then moves on to a manufacturing use case. Chapter 6 focuses on mobile data discovery and looks at a company with a mature sales operation. Chapter 7 covers advanced data acquisition and data processing, including concepts like data wrangling and cleansing and concluding with examples of using the Python programming language to perform data processing.

CHAPTER 2

■ ■ ■

The Salesforce Analytics Cloud Explorer

What I hear I forget, what I see I remember, what I do I know.

—Confucius

The ancient Chinese philosopher Confucius counsels us to be doers, that this is the way to acquire knowledge. If you have read this far, then you likely have more than just a passing interest in the Salesforce Analytics Cloud and data discovery. You may be considering trying the Salesforce Analytics Cloud. The good news is that becoming a doer with the Salesforce Analytics Cloud is not difficult. In fact, using the Salesforce Analytics's Cloud Explorer is exactly what is covered in this chapter.

What Is Cloud Explorer?

The Salesforce Analytics Cloud Explorer—or as we call it, Cloud Explorer—is the user interface. Basically, it is the user experience for the Salesforce Analytics Cloud. It allows users to create data discovery applications by uploading data, creating graphics and dashboards, and bundling these into applications.

Cloud Explorer has two primary server methods for users to access it. The first is a desktop client that runs in a web browser; the second runs via a mobile device. The mobile device can be an Apple iPhone or an Apple iPad. In fact, Apple iPhone users can even use Cloud Explorer on a limited basis on the Apple Watch. And users are not required to employ any of these devices exclusively; a Cloud Explorer user can also create items on the desktop client and view them on an iPhone or iPad.

In this chapter, we examine the Cloud Explorer in detail, explaining its major elements and the capabilities it delivers. In the process, we use Wave with a simple dataset, and we show some presentations of the data with Cloud Explorer. This will give you the best sense of what is possible with Cloud Explorer, and by extension the entire Salesforce Analytics Cloud. We wrap up this chapter with a discussion of Cloud Explorer capabilities to help you decide if the Salesforce Analytics Cloud is right for your uses.

The Two Versions of the Salesforce Analytics Cloud

There are two versions of the Salesforce Analytics Cloud, each targeted to a different audience. Pricing is not being covered here, as prices are subject to change; you should contact your sales representative for answers to questions about pricing. The two versions are as follows.

The Wave Analytics App

This "lite" version of the Salesforce Analytics Cloud allows users to perform data exploration only on Salesforce data. It does not allow users to upload their own data to the Salesforce Analytics Cloud into datasets. This simpler version is intended for sales managers and individuals who only want to use the Salesforce Analytics Cloud with Salesforce data. It is billed as "ready to go" and is very easy to use.

Users of this version are limited to total datasets of 25 million rows. They are, however, permitted to customize their dashboards and share data from Cloud Explorer to Salesforce chatter, or via email.

The Wave Analytics Platform

This version of the Salesforce Analytics Cloud essentially offers full use of the Salesforce Analytics Cloud. Users upload their own data into datasets using either .csv files or a wide array of other methods, including ETL tools. (We will cover ETL tools in Chapter 4.) Programmers can access the application program interfaces (APIs) to load data into the Salesforce Analytics Cloud, and this has a more general data discovery capability; in essence, it can be considered an alternative to data discovery products offered by other vendors. The Wave Analytics Platform is the focus of this book, and all the use cases and examples illustrate how to create items from non-Salesforce data sources.

There is a limit of 100 million total rows of data per user for this platform. Salesforce has bundled 24/7 support with the platform, along with unlimited free training and an assigned "success representative" to ensure customers have a good experience.

Getting Started with Cloud Explorer

Salesforce makes it relatively easy to try Wave, even if you are evaluating the Salesforce CRM on a trial basis. To sample Wave, you must create a permissions group with Wave Analytics privileges, and then assign this permission set to users. This procedure is detailed in Salesforce Wave online help, so we do not cover the steps here.

Launching Cloud Explorer

As soon as permission sets are in place, users can launch Wave Analytics from the Salesforce Applications menu in the upper right corner of the console. This is shown in Figure 2-1.

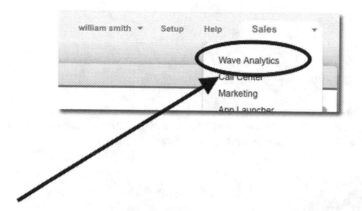

Figure 2-1. *Launching Cloud Explorer from the Salesforce console*

Once the Cloud Explorer starts, you'll see the main screen and can begin using the features of this product. These possibilities are shown in Figure 2-2.

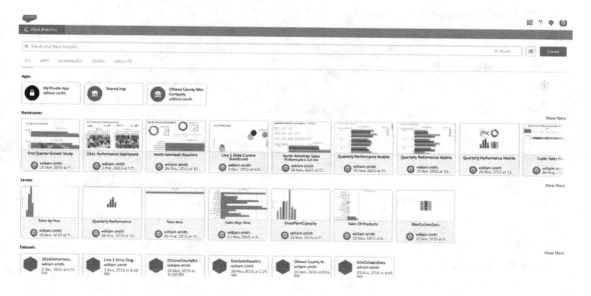

Figure 2-2. *Main screen for Cloud Explorer*

In the middle of the main screen is a box that allows you to search for objects by name. Below the search bar are tabs for the four major objects in Cloud Explorer: datasets, lens, dashboards, and apps.

Datasets are created first. From datasets, lenses are created; the lenses are used to create views of data that are manipulated in the dashboard editor. Be aware that the views of the data will change if the underlying data changes. In the upper right corner of the main screen are two buttons, as shown in closeup view in Figure 2-3.

Figure 2-3. *Buttons from upper right corner of main Cloud Explorer screen*

The button on the left switches to a compact list view of all objects in Cloud Explorer; this list is useful for users with a large number of objects. The button also can be used to switch back to the thumbnail view. The button on the right is used to create datasets and apps, as shown in Figure 2-4.

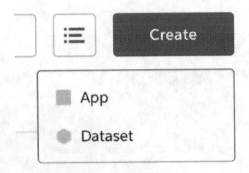

Figure 2-4. *Create button for Cloud Explorer, used for apps or datasets*

Creating a dataset is the first step in using Cloud Explorer and in creating objects. When this button is pressed, you see the screen shown in Figure 2-5.

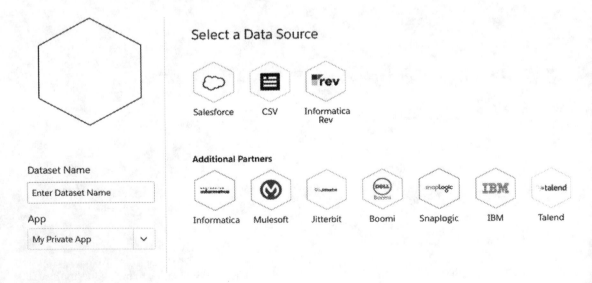

Figure 2-5. *Screen for creating a dataset*

We'll talk more about actually creating a dataset in Chapter 3. For now, let's move on to examine each of the objects types in Cloud Explorer. We begin with datasets.

Datasets

Datasets are the containers for data. All the data used in the Salesforce Analytics Cloud are kept in datasets. These datasets reside on a cloud-based server that operates behind the scenes to provide the data to the Cloud Explorer application. The Wave data server is key to performance; it is capable of quickly ingesting data that consists of thousands of rows—in mere minutes, as it happens. Once a dataset is created, Wave quickly performs the aggregations, filtering, sorting, and rending of that data in real time and supplies it to the Wave user interface.

The data put into the Wave data server is stored in a "faceted" database, whose sole purpose is to support the rapid retrieval of data; above all, it is a responsive user interface. The data put into the Wave server cannot be accessed by any means other than the Wave user interface or APIs. That is, records cannot be modified in the data server. Actually, there are only three operations that can be performed on the Wave data server: creating a dataset, updating a dataset, and deleting a dataset.

Also, data going into Wave has a "one-way ticket." The Wave server is not intended to be of a general-purpose nature; there is really no practical way to run queries against the Wave data server in the same manner as you might with a conventional database server.

Row-Level Security for Datasets

Securing one's data is always a concern regarding databases. Some records might be sensitive and should not be viewed by everyone, for instance. By default, users have access to all the data in a dataset, but Cloud Explorer has a capability for row-level security as a way of restricting access to some records.

To implement row-level security, you define a predicate, or filter, for each dataset on which you want to limit access. We won't cover security predicates in this chapter, but we will touch upon them in Chapter 4.

Lenses

Lenses are views of the data in datasets. Developing views is a multistep process performed within the Cloud Builder, and it is covered in Chapter 3. Once a lens is complete, it can be used alone or can be bundled into a dashboard. To better understand lenses, let's cover the elements of views in some detail.

Measures

The Salesforce Analytics Cloud is oriented toward performing analytics on numeric data. Measures, then, are numeric data that can be aggregated. To get started creating a lens, you first select a measure of interest from your datasets, along with an aggregation. The available aggregations for measures are *sum, average, maximum value, minimum value,* and *unique values.* You also have the ability to create a measure based on *record count* for any measure or dimension.

Measures are created in lenses with the +Measure button, as shown in Figure 2-6. To create the measure, the user selects a measure from the dataset and one of the aggregations.

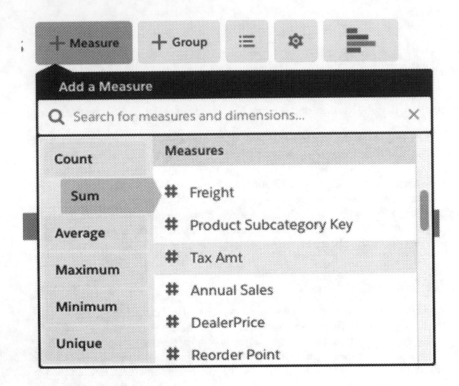

Figure 2-6. *Adding a measure to a lens*

When at least one measure has been selected, you can add dimensions to that lens. Dimensions are covered in the next section.

Dimensions

Dimensions are qualities of the measures; they provide a means for refining and grouping the measures. Dimensions can consist of text or numeric data. When a dataset is created, Cloud Builder will designate all purely numeric columns as measures, but it is possible to change these to dimensions. When a column has been designated as a dimension, it cannot be changed back to a measure, however. Because of this irrevocability, if you want to use a column as both a dimension and a measure, you need to duplicate the column and designate one as a dimension and one as a measure.

To apply a dimension to a lens, you use the +Group button, as shown in Figure 2-7.

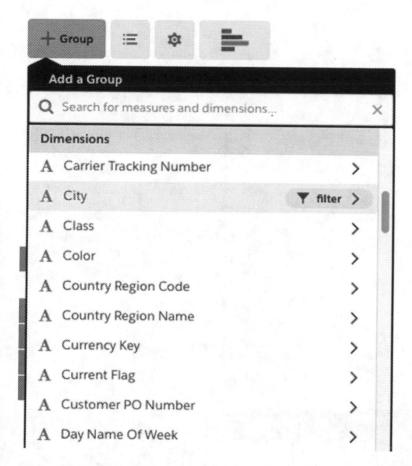

Figure 2-7. *Adding a dimension to a lens*

When dimensions are added to a lens, you can specify a filter by clicking on the Filter button on the right side of the selector message box. Cloud Builder shows the possible values for the filter. For example, a month number filter is shown in Figure 2-8, with months 1 and 2 (January and February) selected.

Figure 2-8. *Add a month dimension to a lens*

Dates

Dates are used in a manner similar to dimensions when creating lenses. However, dates are a special data type in Cloud Explorer. When you select a date to use in grouping your data, you can select a level of granularity. This is illustrated in Figure 2-9.

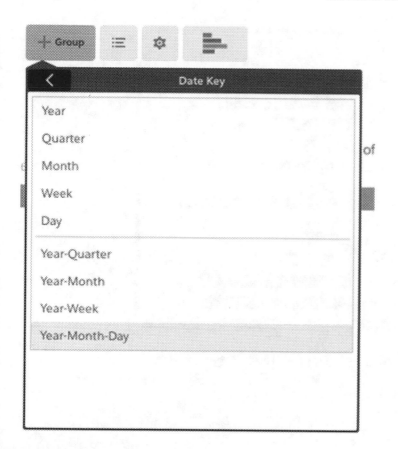

Figure 2-9. *Selecting date options for a lens*

Bringing It All Together

Now let's look at an example of a graphic presentation as it is created in Cloud Builder. The dataset used to build this example graphic is a list of all nuclear power plants in the United States, gathered from a publicly available source. We have chosen the horizontal bar chart, one of the most common graphic presentations. There are two dimensions to the bar chart. The first is the date that the construction permit was issued for the plant to be built. This dataset contains the full date, but for purposes of illustration we have selected just the month and year, indicated by the first three characters of the dimension. There are two three-character values: "pwr" for pressurized water reactor and "bwr" for boiling water reactor. The measure we have chosen is "Licensed Mwt," which indicates the total output power of the power plant in megaWatts. This finished bar chart is shown in Figure 2-10.

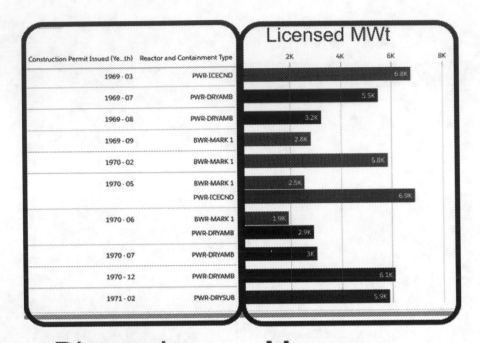

Figure 2-10. *Options for presenting data on nuclear power plants*

If you want to see only the plants that have pressurized water reactors ("pwr"), you can apply a filter to the Reactor and Containment type, as shown in Figure 2-11.

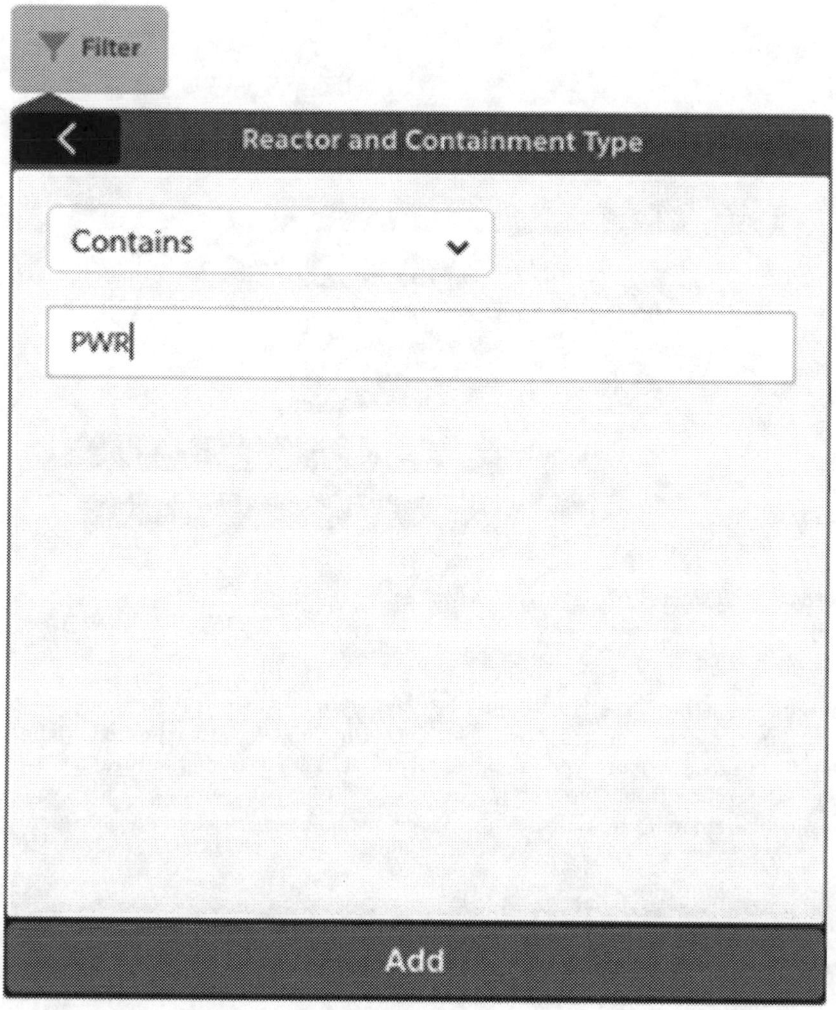

Figure 2-11. *Filter applied to dimension for reactor type*

Now, the graphic will display only a listing of plants with "pwr" as their dimension, shown in Figure 2-12.

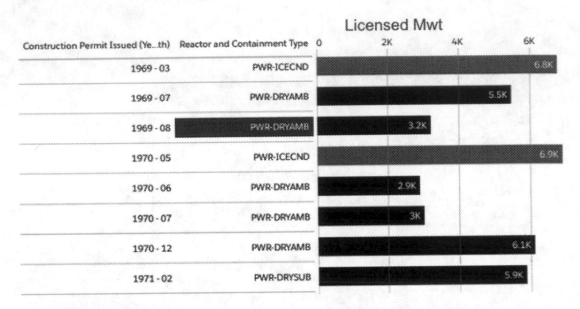

Figure 2-12. *Presentation of data with filter applied for reactor type*

Learn by Doing

Remember the quote from Confucius at the start of this chapter, advising us to be "doers"? Wave makes it easy to experiment with graph types in a lens, and it is instructive to experiment with these types to find the one that best suits your needs. There are also table types, including a raw dump of data, comparison tables, and pivot tables. An example of the comparison table is shown in Figure 2-13. This presentation allows you to change the column names so different measures can be shown together, one as values and one as a graph.

Plant Name, Unit Number	Licensee	Percent Capacity ▾	Megawatt ⌄
Davis-Besse Nuclear Power Stat...t 1	First Energy Nuclear Operating Co.	0.74	2,817
Diablo Canyon Nuclear Power P...t 1	Pacific Gas & Electric Co.	0.87	3,411
Diablo Canyon Nuclear Power P...t 2	Pacific Gas & Electric Co.	0.86	3,411
Donald C. Cook Nuclear Power ...t 1	Indiana Michigan Power Co.	0.94	3,304
Donald C. Cook Nuclear Power ...t 2	Indiana Michigan Power Co.	1.01	3,468
Dresden Nuclear Power Station...t 2	Exelon Generation Co., LLC	0.98	2,957
Dresden Nuclear Power Station...t 3	Exelon Generation Co., LLC	0.95	2,957
Duane Arnold Energy Center	NextEra Duane Arnold, LLC	0.79	1,912
Edwin I. Hatch Nuclear Plant, Unit 1	Southern Nuclear Operating Co.	0.89	2,804
Edwin I. Hatch Nuclear Plant, Unit 2	Southern Nuclear Operating Co.	0.99	2,804
Fermi, Unit 2	DTE Electric Company	0.82	3,486

Figure 2-13. *Comparison table*

Lens Modification History, Undo, and Replay

While you are experimenting with a lens, you can always undo your changes or view the history of your modifications to a lens by using the buttons in the upper left of the Cloud Builder screen. For instance, Figure 2-14 shows the History, Backward, and Forward buttons. Notice that there is a list of all the changes made when you press the History button, and a thumbnail shows the version of the lens associated with the change if you locate your cursor over one of the history items.

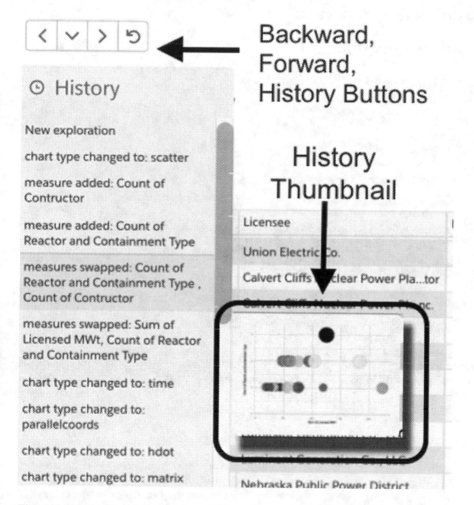

Figure 2-14. Backward, Forward, and History buttons, as well as the lens history thumbnail

Exploring the Data

When you are using a lens, be aware that you can usually click on any value in a chart to reveal a submenu labeled "Drill Into This By...." With this feature, as shown in Figure 2-15, you can select another dimension and further refine your data. Clicking any of the dimensions opens a new version of the lens. Of course, you can return to the prior version by using the Backward button, as mentioned earlier.

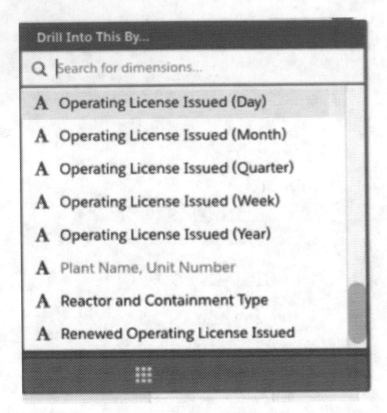

Figure 2-15. Data exploration using the "Drill Into This By..." screen

Mobile Lens Creation

You can create lenses on the iPhone and iPad applications, with capabilities similar to those of the desktop client. This includes the ability to drill into data. Chapter 6 features a use case that shows how to exploit the mobile capabilities of the Salesforce Analytics Cloud.

Dashboards

Cloud Explorer's dashboards enable you to combine multiple graphs or other visualizations of data into a single view. The dashboards include a grid editor focused on aesthetics, thereby enabling you to make presentations that are visually appealing and useful in presentations to customers.

You can also use the dashboards to facilitate any exploration of data. When you make a selection on a widget of a dashboard, it enables you to refine the data, and this change is reflected on all other dashboard widgets. This feature is demonstrated at several points in this book, so you'll be able to see this feature in action. Now let's examine some of the widgets that are available on the dashboards.

Widgets

By way of explanation, widgets of various types are the tools of a dashboard. Figure 2-16 shows the widgets that can be found in Cloud Builder.

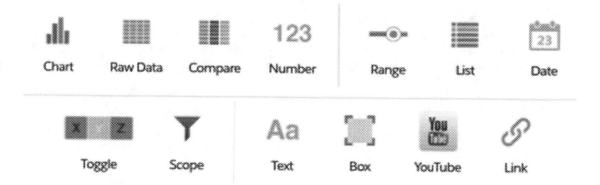

Figure 2-16. *Widgets available in Cloud Builder*

There are three basic types of widgets: those for data display, for selector choice, and for display.

Data Display Widgets

These widgets are all used to display data that originates in a lens. They have differing capabilities based on their purpose, so some widgets work with many measures while others work with only one measure.

Chart Widget

The chart widget has the same array of chart types as are available when you build lenses. You can change the chart type at any time when you are building a dashboard, so you are not restricted to the chart type used to build the lens.

When you select a widget, a properties window appears on the right side of the Cloud Builder screen. There is a default property labeled "faceted." If you de-select "faceted" for a widget, the data on the widget will not change as you apply any refinements with other widgets. The faceted property is shown in Figure 2-17.

Figure 2-17. *The faceted property is selected by default*

Raw Data Widget

As its name implies, this widget allows you to view a spreadsheet-style table of data from a lens. You can remove columns as desired, change the position of the columns, and sort the table with data from a column. To use the raw data widget in a dashboard, you must first create a lens with the raw data widget.

Compare Table Widget

An example of a comparison table was shown in Figure 2-13. Be aware that the comparison table has the same requirement as the raw data widget. You must first create a compare data widget in a lens before it can be used in a dashboard.

Number Widget

The number widget is used to display a single value on a dashboard. To use the number widget, you must create a lens with a measure and aggregation, and with no groups or dimensions applied. Numbers are useful to display summary data like total sales or some other grand total.

Toggle Widget

The toggle widget is both a selector for a dimension and a display widget for a measure. It can be used to apply a refinement to a dimension, and it can also display aggregated data associated with the dimension. The toggle widget is one of the most versatile and powerful widgets, used extensively in the examples given in this book.

Selector Widgets

The following widgets provide intuitive methods to refine data, based on the data type.

Date Widget

Date widgets are used to select a date range, and they must be used with date data from a lens. The date widget is a powerful selection tool because it allows many different ways to select a date, as can be seen in Figure 2-18, including by quarter, month, or week.

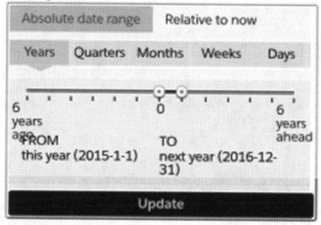

Figure 2-18. Date Widget

Range Widget

The range widget is shown in Figure 2-19. It is used to select a numeric range to refine a measure. To use the range widget, you must create a lens with a measure and aggregation, and no groups or dimensions applied.

Sales Amount

From	To
4,621.642	27,893.619

Figure 2-19. Range widget

Display Widgets

These widgets are for display only and can only be modified at design time.

Scope Widget

The scope widget displays filters applied on lens data. It does not allow filter criteria to be changed, and is only a display mechanism. Figure 2-20 shows the scope widget, with a filter applied to date data to select quarter 1, and a filter applied to a region dimension to select only the United States and Canada.

Calendar Quarter	Sales Territory Country	Calendar Quarter	Sales Territory Country
Equals 1	Equals Canada, United States	Equals 1	Equals Canada, United States

Figure 2-20. Scope widget

Text Widget

The text widget allows you to add a title to a dashboard, instructions, or comments on the data. You can use this widget to change the font size and the text color.

Box Widget

The box widget allows you to add a shaded area to a dashboard and to visually group widgets together, or to highlight some aspect of the dashboard.

The Dashboard Development Cycle

All dashboards are built on lens data, and you must first develop a lens to produce a view of the data before it can be used by a dashboard widget. This workflow is demonstrated in Chapter 3, but we will quickly summarize it here.

When you have found your data in Cloud Builder, you use the button in the upper right corner of the Cloud Builder screen to "clip" the data and make it available to a dashboard. This button is shown in Figure 2-21.

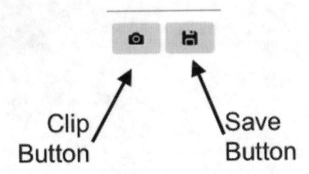

Figure 2-21. The Clip and Save buttons

Note that both the dashboard and the lens builders have a Save button. You should use it frequently to save your changes to your dashboards or lenses. Be aware that changes in Cloud Builder are not automatically saved, so if you do not use the Save button frequently, you could lose work. Also, be aware that saving a lens only saves the query associated with the lens; it does not preserve a snapshot of the data.

Once you have clipped your lens, you proceed to the dashboard editor to use the lens data. When you clip a lens, if a dashboard associated with the lens does not already exist, then a new dashboard will be created. You can view all of the lens data in a dashboard with the control on the left side of the dashboard, as shown in Figure 2-22. From this control, you can delete any lens data that is not used by a widget, and you can select the lens data to be used by a widget.

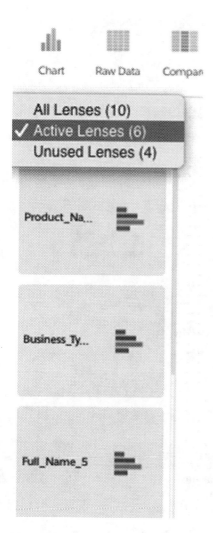

Figure 2-22. *Lens data browser in dashboard builder*

To use the lens data, select a widget from tool bar; it will appear on the dashboard builder. Lenses whose data can be used with the widget will be highlighted in the lens data browser. You select the lens whose data you would like to use and drag it to the widget. This is illustrated in Figure 2-23 and is also described in more detail in Chapter 3.

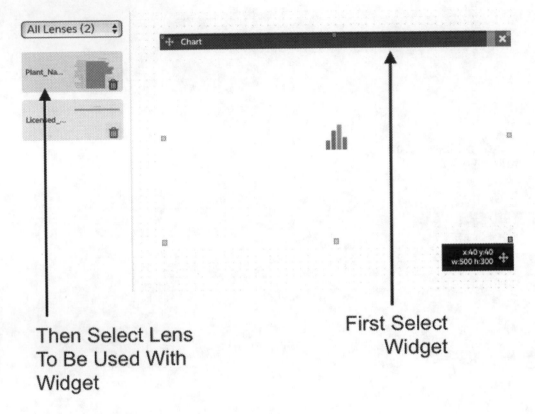

Then Select Lens To Be Used With Widget

First Select Widget

Figure 2-23. Associating the lens data with a widget

Link Back to Lens

On dashboards, widgets have a button that allows you to link back to the lens used with the widget. This button is shown in Figure 2-24. Clicking this button immediately opens the lens for review. It is a useful tool when creating a new lens, based on the same lens used in a dashboard.

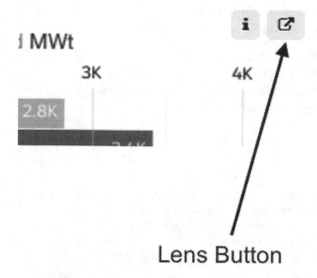

Figure 2-24. *Lens button for reviewing previous lens*

You can disable the Lens button, and there are several reasons for doing so. For example, you may want to prevent users from inadvertently clicking it or from perusing the lens data. The disable attribute for the Lens button is shown in Figure 2-25.

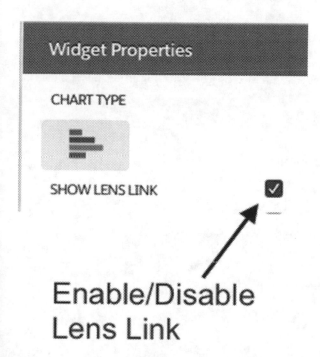

Figure 2-25. *Enable/disable Lens button*

You may have noticed the button with an "i" in Figure 2-23. You use this button to display information about the lens for a widget.

Dashboard Wrap-Up

With the information covered in this section, you should be able to begin creating your own dashboards. There's more information on the dashboards in Chapter 3. Chapters 5 and 6 have use cases that show the use of dashboards.

Apps

The final major element of Cloud Explorer is its apps. The apps allow you to bundle the dashboards, lenses, and datasets. These apps do not have inherent features beyond their container function, so there are no editors for them. Apps are created with the Create button, shown earlier in Figure 2-4.

When you use the Save button for objects, you can associate them with an app. Datasets can be associated with an app by editing them, then changing their app. An app can contain any number of datasets, dashboards, and lenses.

My Private App

There is a default app in Cloud Explorer called My Private App. As its name implies, no other users can see anything in this app. This is the default Save location for all objects, and it's a staging area or scratchpad that you should use to store objects before they are ready for public consumption.

The Share Button

Apps, lenses, and dashboards all have a Share button that you have no doubt noticed by now. The Share button is used to share objects with others who have Salesforce logins. The Share button for apps is shown in Figure 2-26.

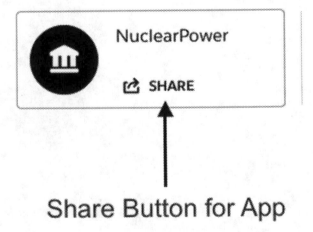

Figure 2-26. *The Share button for apps*

The Share button will open the message box shown in Figure 2-27. The features of this message box are common means for sharing and collaborating, allowing you to select individual users for sharing or levels of persons in your organization. For example, you can post to your Salesforce feed, take a screenshot, and get a URL that you can share with those you have allowed to view the app. This collaborative capability makes sharing your data discovery work in the Salesforce Analytics Cloud quite simple. Note that sharing a screenshot creates a graphic snapshot that can be shared with those who are not Salesforce Analytics Cloud users. Sharing a dashboard or lens with these users is not possible, however.

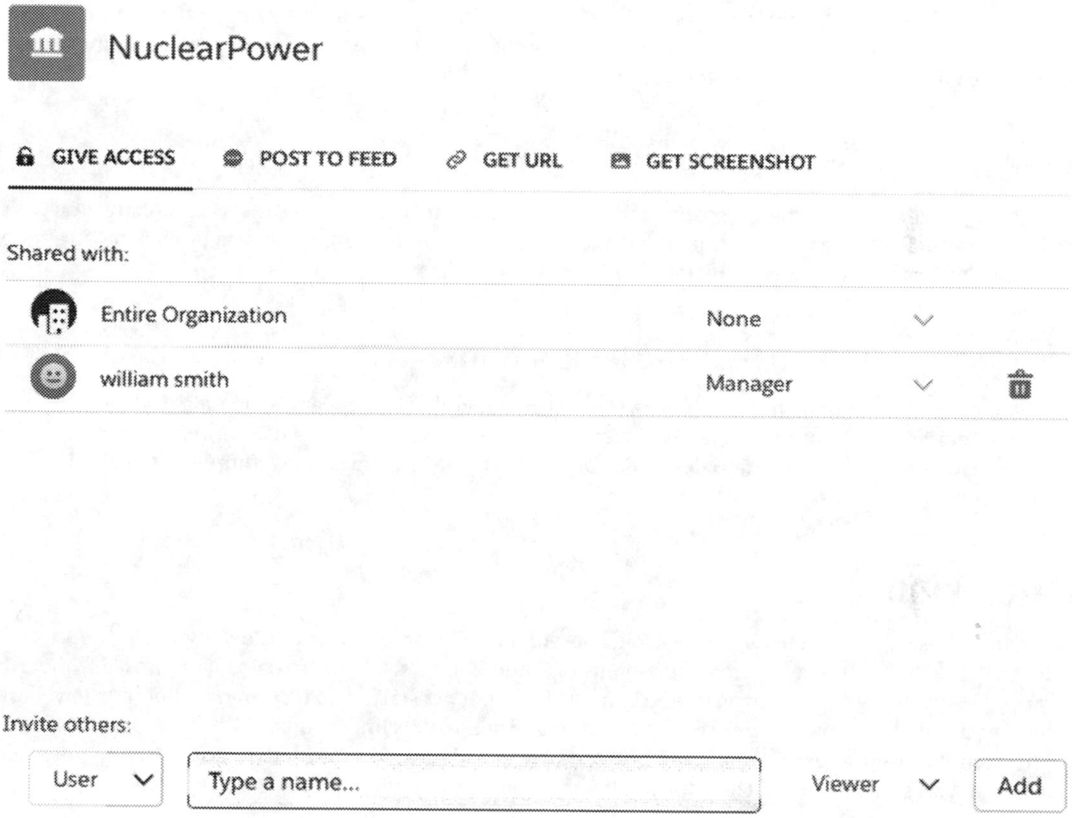

Figure 2-27. Sharing options for an app

Playground Data

Cloud Explorer has access to "playground data" on mobile devices that you can use to get familiar with Cloud Explorer. This data consists of different applications, so you see good examples of all of its elements.

What Wave Lacks

You may be in the process of evaluating Wave as a data discovery product, so it is important to point out aspects that may be deal breakers.

Text Processing and Analysis

Wave is a product that at its core is capable of performing only basic aggregations on numeric data. It has no capability to perform text processing and it lacks visualizations for text analysis, like tag clouds. Wave can use text as a dimension in its visualizations, but in this context its purpose is only to provide meaning to numeric data.

To illustrate this point, if you have a simple spreadsheet that ranks cars on their quarter-mile times by make and model, then the names of the cars would simply be present as a legend or axis label on a graph against numeric data. Wave has no capability of performing presentations with the names of the cars. Wave also lacks the capability of performing a search on text data. So if your dataset is a huge list of cars produced over sixty years, you will not have an ability to search for the name for any car. However, you can filter on text, and in some circumstances this may suit your needs.

Map and Geospatial Data

Wave has no means of handling geospatial data in its visual controls or widgets. If you are looking for a data discovery product with a map component that allows selection and refinement of data by clicking on a map, then you might want to consider a different data discovery product.

Advanced Math and Statistical Functions

Advanced math functions are not available in Wave. This capability is not featured in data discovery products in general, so if you are designing an application or workflow that needs a more complex mathematical function, like standard deviations or moving averages, you should compute these on data before loading it into Wave.

Conclusion

This chapter has examined the most user-facing part of the Salesforce Analytics Cloud, which is Cloud Explorer. Presented here were the major elements of Cloud Explorer, which are datasets, lenses, dashboards, and apps. Also provided was information to help the beginner get started using Cloud Explorer, followed by a review of the sharing capabilities of Cloud Explorer and some of its limitations.

Remember the advice of Confucius to be a "doer" to gain knowledge. With the information presented in this chapter, you can take the first step toward being a doer with Cloud Explorer.

■ ■ ■

CHAPTER 3

Analytics Cloud Builder

Intuition becomes increasingly valuable in the new information society precisely because there is so much data.

—John Naisbitt

American author and speaker John Naisbitt is highly recognized in his studies of future trends. He extended Einstein's conclusion that "The only real valuable thing is intuition" by emphasizing the importance of human intuition in the era of data explosion and abundance. An intuitive user interface to explore data and develop visualization is of critical value, and that's one of key benefits of Salesforce Analytics Cloud.

In Chapter 2, we covered various visualizations available in Salesforce Analytics Cloud. In this chapter, we will focus on designing dashboards using the Analytics Cloud Builder.

We will first create a step-by-step dashboard from scratch with one simple dataset. We will then cover topics concerning best practices to design visualization. Creating dataset and dashboard through mobile device will also be demonstrated, followed by advanced dashboard development using SAQL.

Building a Simple Dashboard

In this section, we will first go through a step-by-step dashboard building exercise. All datasets and JSON templates can be downloaded from www.apress.com/9781484212042 and clicking on the Source Code tab. You can follow along the examples as we step through.

Loading Dataset

The dataset we are using is a .csv file from a FAA public database recording bird strikes statistics. It contains information on each recorded bird strike including accident airport, altitude, aircraft make and model, location, flight date and time, damage, airline, origin state, phase of flight, weather condition, wildlife size, and species, etc.

Figure 3-1 is a screenshot of the raw dataset in Microsoft Excel. Note that not all columns of data are shown.

	A	B	C	D	E	F
1	Aircraft: Type	Airport: Name	Altitude bin	Aircraft: Make/Model	Wildlife: Number struck	Effect: Impact to flight
2	Airplane	NEWARK LIBERTY INTL ARPT	< 1000 ft	B-757-200	2 to 10	
3	Airplane	UNKNOWN	Unknown	B-737-300	1	
4	Airplane	DENVER INTL AIRPORT	Unknown	B-737-300	1	
5	Airplane	CHICAGO O'HARE INTL ARPT	Unknown	B-727-200	1	
6		JOHN F KENNEDY INTL	Unknown	UNKNOWN	1	
7	Airplane	UNKNOWN	< 1000 ft	C-550	1	Other
8	Airplane	UNKNOWN	< 1000 ft	B-727-200	1	None
9	Airplane	CINCINNATI MUNI ARPT-LUNKEN FIELD	< 1000 ft	CITATION II	1	None
10	Airplane	MIAMI INTL	> 1000 ft	DA-2000	1	None
11	Airplane	SAN FRANCISCO INTL ARPT	< 1000 ft	B-737-500	1	
12	Airplane	SALT LAKE CITY INTL	< 1000 ft	B-737-300	2 to 10	Other
13		MIAMI INTL	Unknown	UNKNOWN	2 to 10	
14	Airplane	SOUTHWEST FLORIDA INTL ARPT	< 1000 ft	HAWKER 800	1	None
15	Airplane	KANSAS CITY INTL	< 1000 ft	MD-80	11 to 100	None
16	Airplane	NASHVILLE INTL	< 1000 ft	B-737-400	1	None
17	Airplane	SAN ANTONIO INTL	Unknown	B-737	1	Precautionary Landi

Figure 3-1. *Raw Bird Strike dataset*

We use Analytics Cloud's data loader User Interface (UI) to upload the dataset into the system. Here are the steps:

1. Click on "Create" button on the top right corner of screen from the Analytics Explorer homepage. Press "App" and create an app called "Book Apps." Then press the "Create" button again and select "Dataset" (see Figure 3-2.)

Figure 3-2. *Create app and dataset*

2. Click on the "CSV" button under the "Select a Data Source" menu (see Figure 3-3).

Select a Data Source

Salesforce   CSV   Informatica
                            Rev

Additional Partners

Informatica   Mulesoft   Jitterbit   Boomi   Snaplogic   IBM   Talend

Figure 3-3. *Select data source*

3. Enter "Bird Strike" in the textbox for "Dataset Name." Select the name of the app in the dropdown list where you want the dataset to reside. In this case, we have created an app called "Book Apps." Recall that we covered using the "create" button to create apps in chapter 2. Click on "Select file or drag files here" and navigate to the dataset location. The system will automatically generate a metadata file in JSON format, which you can download and modify as needed. Or you can upload your own metadata file as the definition of the dataset (see Figure 3-4).

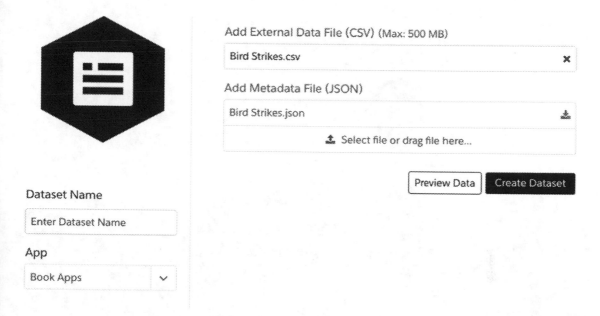

Add External Data File (CSV) (Max: 500 MB)

Bird Strikes.csv ✕

Add Metadata File (JSON)

Bird Strikes.json ⬇

⬆ Select file or drag file here...

Preview Data   Create Dataset

Dataset Name

Enter Dataset Name

App

Book Apps ⌄

Figure 3-4. *Enter metadata for dataset*

4.   Click on "Create Dataset" button and your dataset will be uploaded into the Analytics Cloud. Datasets are usually created immediately, but there is usually a message that reads "Your dataset will be created within the hour.

5.   Once the system finishes data loading process, your dataset will show up on the Analytics Cloud Explorer for use. You can navigate to the dataset either through the application wrapper you've created it under or by clicking on the "DATASETS" tab on the top. Click on the "Bird Strikes" dataset to view the new dataset (see Figure 3-5).

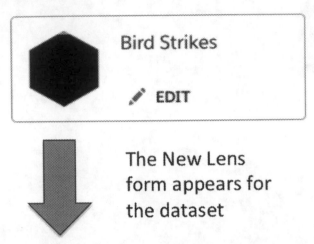

Select "Bird Strikes" dataset

Bird Strikes

✏ EDIT

The New Lens form appears for the dataset

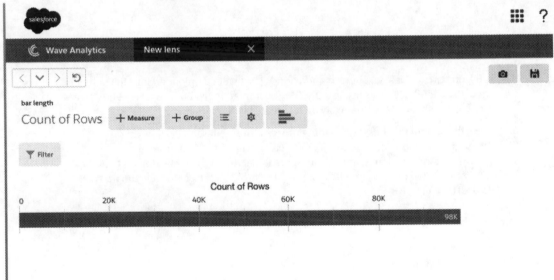

Figure 3-5. *Select "Bird Stikes" dataset to view dataset*

Creating a Dashboard

Now that the dataset is uploaded, it's time to explore the data by creating our dashboard. The first step is to create lenses that will build up our dashboard. Below are the step-by-step instructions on how to create a lens and how to include it in the dashboard designer.

1. We start with clicking on the dataset "Bird Strikes" we created in the last section of this chapter. We click on the "+Group" button and select "Conditions: Sky" from the Dimensions list (see Figure 3-6).

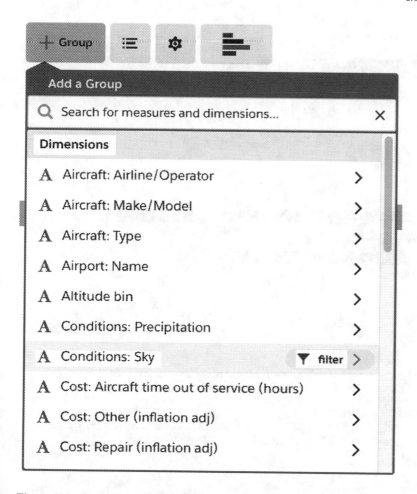

Figure 3-6. *Create group by condition: sky*

2. The chart shown in Figure 3-7 will be displayed based on the number of unique values in the "Conditions: Sky" dimension.

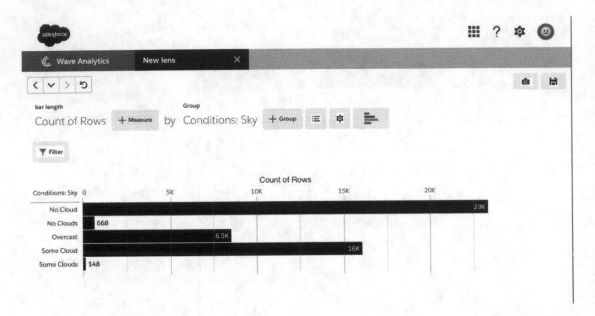

Figure 3-7. *Lens group by sky condition*

3. Click on the camera button on the top right corner of the screen. The lens you just created will be "clipped" into the dashboard designer.

4. In the dashboard designer screen (Figure 3-8), you'll see the lens you clipped on the left panel. Click on the "Toggle" widget type on the top widget bar, and then click on the lens on the left side to add "Conditions_Sky_1" lens into the Toggle widget.

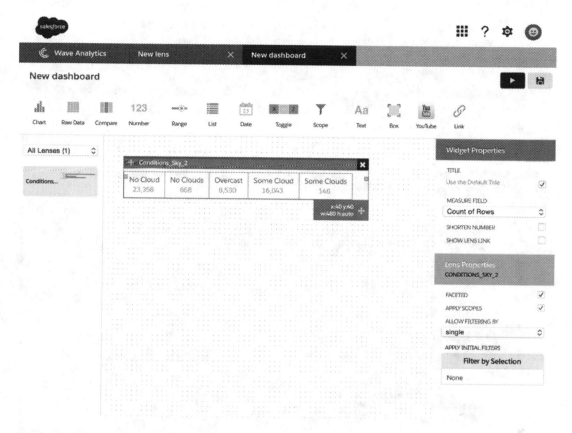

Figure 3-8. *Sky condition toggle widget*

5. Go back to the lens tab (Figure 3-9), click on "Condition: Sky" grouping and replace it with "When: Time of Day" dimension. This is done by removing the "Condition: Sky" grouping. Hover over the grouping, and click the "x" in the upper right corner of the grouping. Then click the "+Group" button and add "When: Time of Day."

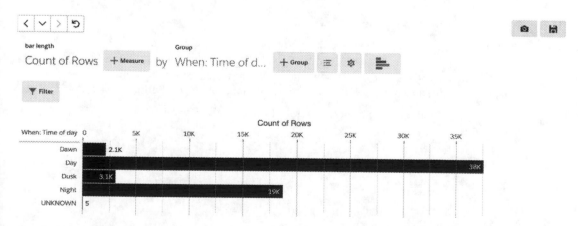

Figure 3-9. *Lens group by time of day*

6. Repeat steps 3 and 4 to clip the new lens "When_Time_of_Day_2" into the designer. Add it to a new Toggle widget to the right of the first Toggle button. Note that newly clipped lenses are always at the top of the lens stack shown on the left side of the dashboard designer.

7. Go back to the lens tab, click on the grouping button and replace it with "Wildlife: Size." Change the visualization type to a donut chart (see Figure 3-10).

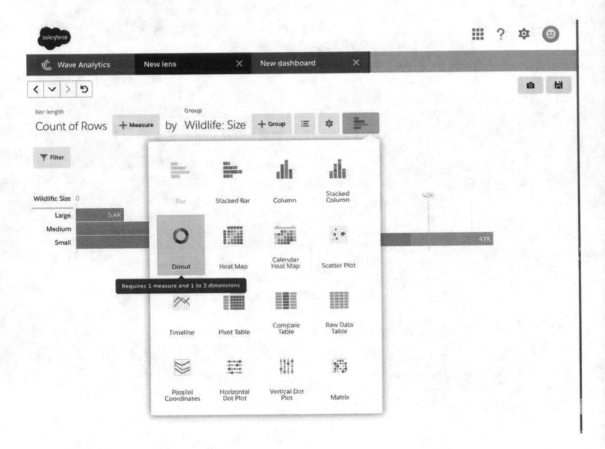

Figure 3-10. *Lens chart for wildlife size*

8. Repeat steps 3 and 4 to clip the lens into dashboard designer. Choose a "Chart" widget type this time and place it under the "Condition: Sky" toggle button.

9. Repeat steps 7 and 8 to create another donut chart to display "Wildlife: Species" breakdown.

Define filters to exclude "unknown" types of animal species. To create the exclude filter, click on filter "Wildlife: Species", and scroll to the bottom of the list. You will see "more" at the bottom of the list. Click on more to list more species. Scroll to the bottom of the list again, and click more. Repeat scrolling and clicking more, until you are at the end of the list. At the top of the filter this is a control that is used to select "All" items. Click this, to select all species. Scroll to the species and deselect all items that begin with "unknown." This is shown in Figure 3-11.

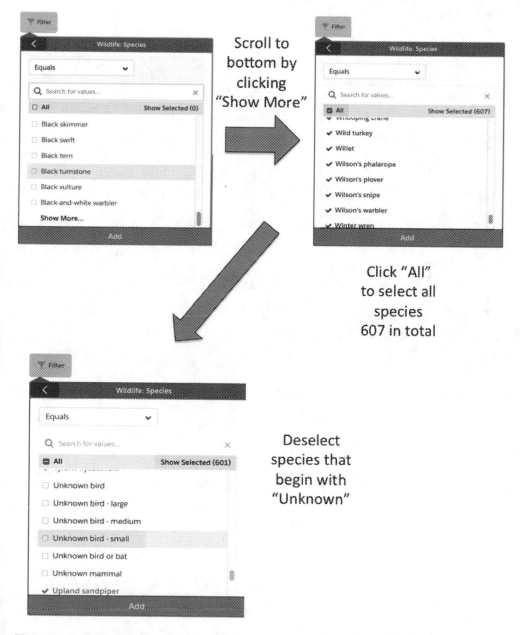

Figure 3-11. *Filter unknown species*

Define another filter to include the species that have more than 100 occurrences of incidents. Press the filter button, select count of rows, and "Greater Than Or Equal To." Then enter 100, and click "Add." (See Figure 3-12)

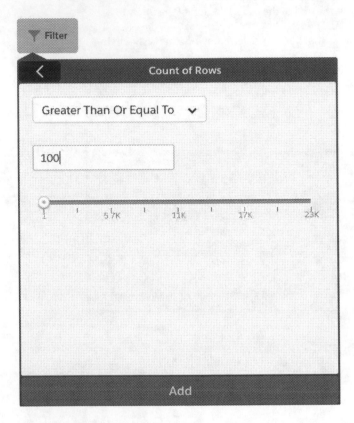

Figure 3-12. *Set number of incidents >=100*

Figure 3-13 shows the lens after filters and all filters have been applied.

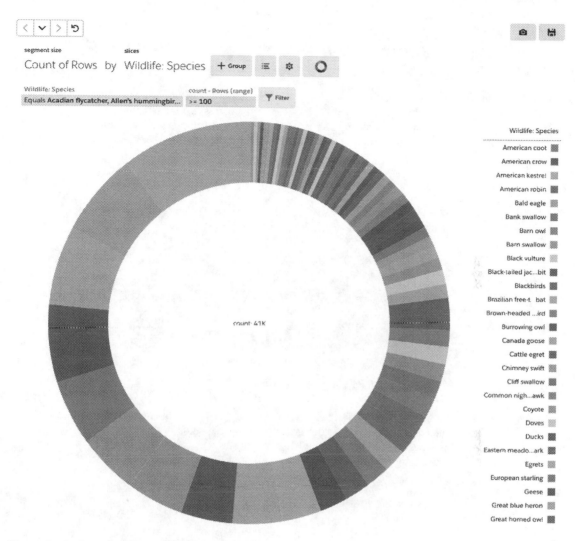

Figure 3-13. *Lens chart for wildlife species*

10. By now, you should be comfortable modifying a lens to add new dimensions and clip the lens, like was demonstrated in steps 7 and 8. Repeat this process to add a lens and chart widget for aircraft and pilot information as shown in Figure 3-14. Note that you should use a horizontal bar chart and not the donut visualization in the lens builder.

Create all four vertical charts for the following measures:

- Average of Speed (IAS) in knots

- Max of Speed (IAS) in knots

- Avg of Miles from Airport

- Max of Miles from Airport

And the following dimensions:

- Pilot warned of birds or wildlife?

- Altitude bin

Once this lens is built, clip and add to the dashboard at the bottom. Note that all four horizontal charts are clipped. Only one chart widget is needed to contain these in the dashboard designer. This approach of group multiple widgets in the lens builder is a useful grouping technique when building dashboards.

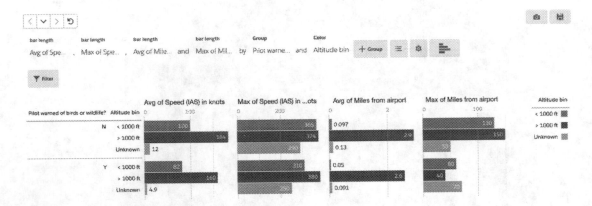

Figure 3-14. *Chart widgets for aircraft and pilot information*

11. The layout of the dashboard designer now looks like this as seen in Figure 3-15. On the right side of the dashboard designer are properties selector that appear whenever a widget is selected. Use the "Display Legend" selector to show the legend for each donut chart.

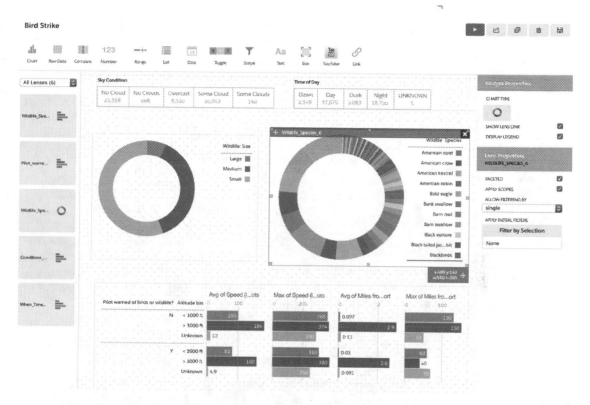

Figure 3-15. *Bird Strike dashboard designer view*

12. Click on the green "Run" button and Figure 3-16 shows the final product of the "Bird Strike" dashboard.

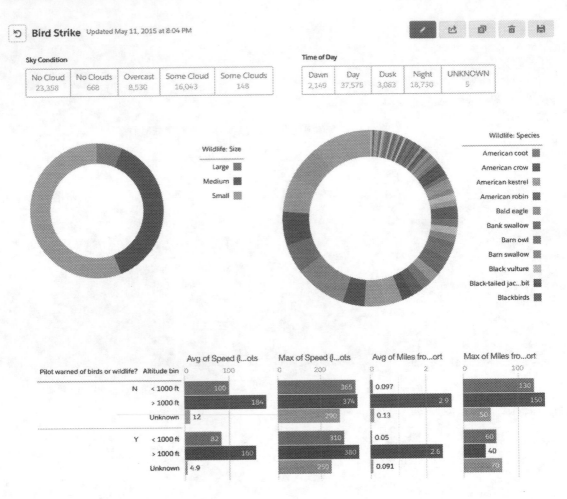

Figure 3-16. *Dashboard view for Bird Strike*

The entire dashboard requires no more than 15 minutes to create for someone familiar with the data used. You can also use grouping and measure features in lens screens to explore the data in the case you are not familiar with what's contained in the dataset. These easy-to-use methods are very intuitive to discover hidden trends of the data including the high-level cardinality, distribution of attributes, and unexpected correlations.

Dashboard Design Aesthetics

We are now familiar with how to create a simple dashboard and explore data in Salesforce Analytics Cloud. In the following section, we will examine dashboard design fundamentals.

Steps to Design Aesthetic Dashboards

Salesforce prides itself on creating superb customer experience. The Salesforce Analytics Cloud is no exception. As we have seen in various examples so far, the visualization capabilities of the Salesforce Analytics Cloud are appealing and the animation when you interact with the system is simply stunning. However, visualizations alone do not make great dashboard and analytics solutions. In this section, we'll cover some tips and best practices on designing effective and meaningful analytics output.

Understand the User Problems

BI developers and analysts frequently make mistakes in determining usage scenarios for their applications, and focusing on metrics that lack relevance or analytic value. The good news is that Salesforce Analytics Cloud is primarily self-servicing in nature. Business analysts can explore datasets, design visualization, and share output all through an intuitive user interface. However, there are circumstances you might be designing a dashboard for use by members of your team.

In order to design effective output, the first step is to understand the business drivers and determine what your users care about. Instead of guessing about what your users will find important, poll them directly to find out the key information needs. Many modern social network sites such as Facebook used this strategy to understand the needs of their advertisers and release UI updates based on the feedback.

User Goals

User experience design should not take on a static method, as human beings are different in what information we need and how we consume what's presented to us. What works for one person might not work for another. The most effective approach is to anticipate specific experiences and to shape certain behaviors. In addition, a well-throughout design must be tailored to the goals, values, and decision process of different personas or user groups.

Usability

User experience and usability have become synonymous, but they are two different concepts. User experience addresses how a user feels when using a system, while usability is about the user-friendliness and efficiency of the interface.

Usability and user experience are not completely unrelated either. Usability is a big part of the user experience and plays an important role in experiences that are effective and pleasant. In addition to usability, human factors, psychology, information architecture and user-centered design principles also have significant impact on the user experience in general.

Design Principles

Here are some of the basic design principles to consider when designing great user experience for analytics solutions.

Principle #1: Ensure readability. Use high contrast for text and background. For example, black text on white or pale yellow backgrounds makes it more consumable. In addition, font sizes should be large enough to be readable on standard displays.

Principle #2: Consider form factor. The size of the font and chart display should be based on the device. Design visualization and display differently and define default and preferred layout for an iPad, iPhone, and web.

Principle #3: Emphasize with visuals. Favor particularly large characters for the actual data you intend to display as opposed to labels and instructions. The way we process information is guided by how it's presented to us. Use boldface, size, density, and movement effectively to activate our visual sensitivity. Try to use charts instead of tables of numbers. Remember, a picture is worth a thousand words and every word is a picture.

Principle #4: Consider age factor. Avoid using younger audience to make size and contrast decisions. Instead, test all designs on the oldest user population you might be expecting. Presbyopia, a condition of gradual loss of our eyes' ability to focus on nearby objects, is a natural, often annoying part of aging. Presbyopia usually becomes noticeable in our early to mid-40s and continues to worsen until around age 65. Be mindful of age differences in visual consumption needs.

Principle #5: Choose simple fonts. Cursive Fonts that are considered aesthetically pleasing suffers lack of readability. Human eyes tend to respond better to sharp edges. As a result, anti-aliasing fonts with softened edge should be avoided, especially in smaller font sizes.

Principle #6: Be smart with layout and display order. Focus on key metrics and gradually descend into higher level of details. Align similar charts for comparison purposes. Balance top down vs. bottom up thinking with overviews of KPI on top and smart use of alerts to drive actions

Principle #7: Avoid common mistakes of jumping to tools first without understanding actual requirements. Another common pitfall is to think within the constraints of traditional BI tools thus limiting the power of data exploration and discovery capabilities.

Principle #8: Choose a good photo or image. Pictures tell a story better than a thousand words, so it is important that you choose a good image for your dashboards. Use cohesive, single image and don't use photos that are collages of other small photos. In addition, try to use an image that has maximum 3-4 colors and shades. Otherwise, it becomes a distraction. Use crisp images. Header image on the sample dashboard is 1420 px by 150 px with 300 ppi resolution. Avoid using images with less resolution. Don't stretch an image, as it'll create distortion and distraction. If you are adding text or numbers on these images, provide a background with sufficient contrast so that the text is legible.

Mobile Dashboard Designer

With these design principles in mind, let's take a look at the mobile dashboard designer. Salesforce Analytics Cloud is mobile-ready on day one. Lenses and dashboards are available on mobile devices such as iPad, iPhone, and Apple Watch with simple page layout configurations. In addition, mobile devices are not just visualization vehicles. You can also perform build and design functions using mobile devices including dataset upload and dashboard design. In this section, we'll walk you through a step-by-step use case of using mobile device to create dashboard through datasets.

Upload Dataset Through Mobile Device

There are a number of ways you can upload a dataset into Analytics Cloud using your mobile device. It can be done through email attachment, files in cloud services such as Dropbox or Salesforce Files. We'll show you how to use Dropbox to upload a dataset into Analytics Cloud in our example.

1. Open "Dropbox" App on your iPhone, and navigate to folder with "Infant Mortality.csv" (see Figure 3-17).

No SIM 📶   7:15 AM   @ ✈ ⁕ 54% ▮▮▮ ⚡

‹ Chapter 3 - HSUN **data**   ⬆   ⋯

📄 Infant Mortality.csv
    7.3 KB, modified 7 months ago

🕐   📄   🖼   ⬇   ⚙
Recents   Files   Photos   Offline   Settings

Figure 3-17. *Dropbox application with files used in this chapter*

    2.   In the Dropbox display screen shown in Figure 3-17, select the file named "Infant Mortality" The file info screen will be displayed (see Figure 3-18).

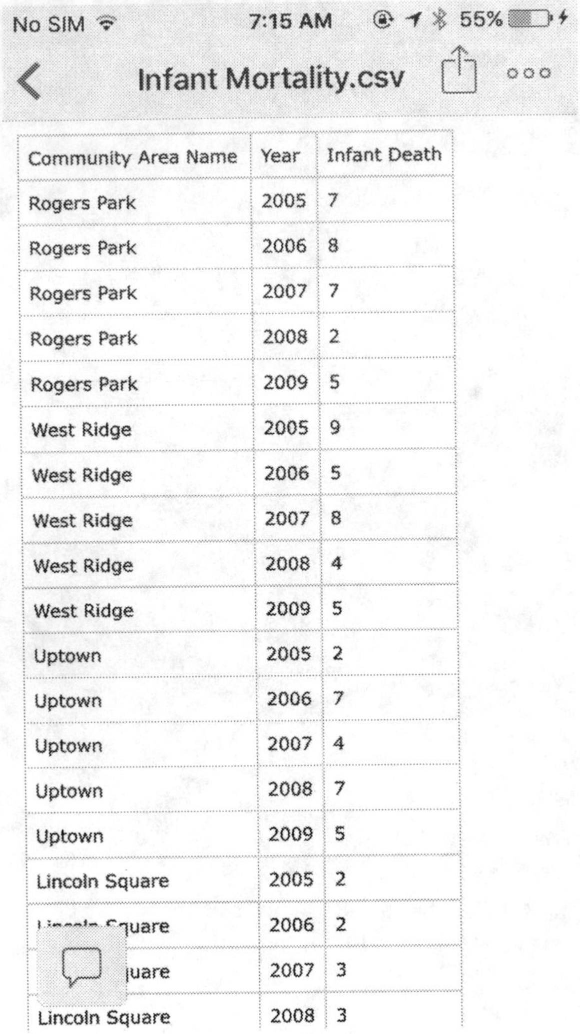

No SIM 🗢   7:15 AM   @ ⤳ ⁎ 55% 🔋⫶

⟨   Infant Mortality.csv   ⬆   ○○○

Community Area Name	Year	Infant Death
Rogers Park	2005	7
Rogers Park	2006	8
Rogers Park	2007	7
Rogers Park	2008	2
Rogers Park	2009	5
West Ridge	2005	9
West Ridge	2006	5
West Ridge	2007	8
West Ridge	2008	4
West Ridge	2009	5
Uptown	2005	2
Uptown	2006	7
Uptown	2007	4
Uptown	2008	7
Uptown	2009	5
Lincoln Square	2005	2
Lincoln Square	2006	2
Lincoln Square	2007	3
Lincoln Square	2008	3

Figure 3-18. *File info view*

3. In the file info screen shown in Figure 3-18, tap the icon ⬆ in the upper right corner of the screen and select "Copy to Wave Analytics" icon as shown in Figure 3-19.

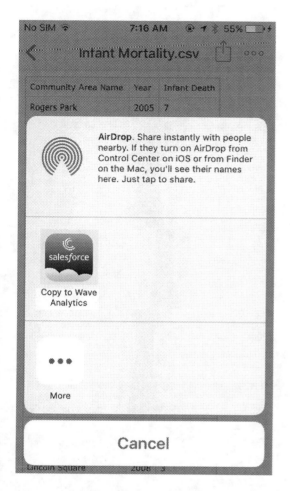

Figure 3-19. *Upload file into Salesforce Analytics Cloud*

4. A data connector popup appears as shown in Figure 3-20. You can scroll indicate that you do not want to see this again. On Figure 3-20, press "next."

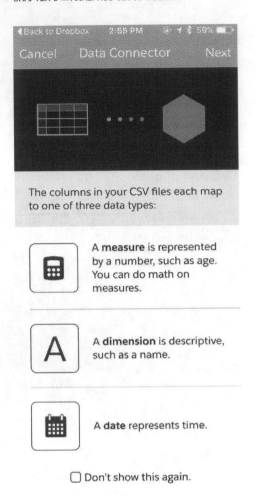

Figure 3-20. *Data connector popup*

5.   Change the Field Type to "Dimension" for "Year" attribute. See Figure 3-21.

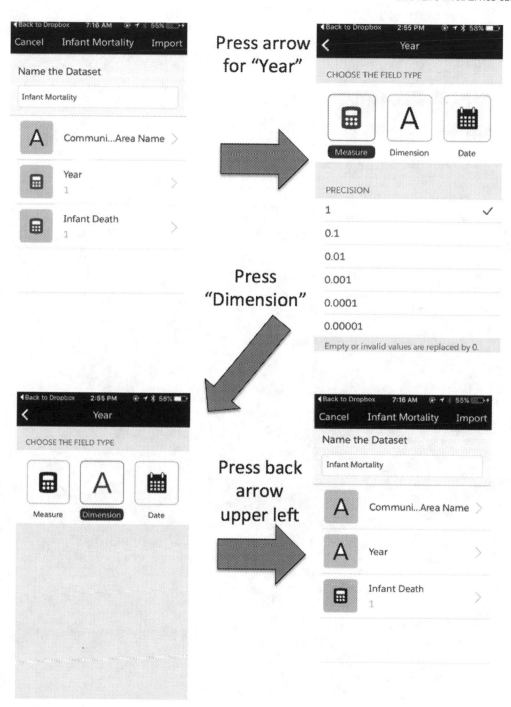

Figure 3-21. *Change year from measure to dimension*

6. Set the name of the dataset to "Infant Mortality" and tap on "Import" see Figure 3-21. Import process begins, as shown in Figure 3-22. Tap done when import completes.

Figure 3-22. *Import complete*

7. After you press "Done" you will see the dataset created. See Figure 3-23. Press the "i" next to the dataset name to see options to open a lens by pressing "Open" or "Create" to a start the dashboard designer. Press "Create" to prepare for the next exercise in this chapter which involves creating a mobile dashboard.

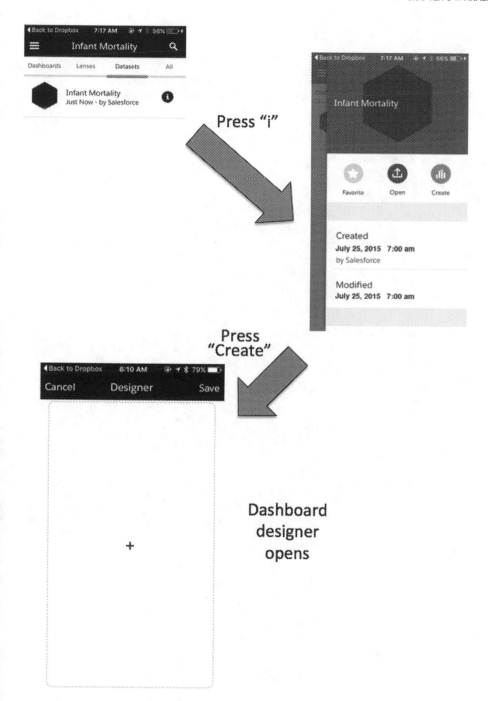

Figure 3-23. *Dataset read for use, press create to start dashboard designer*

Create Dashboard Using Mobile Designer

Now that the dataset is created, it's time to create the dashboard.

1. You can close out the exploration screen and navigate to the "Infant Mortality" dataset. Press and hold the dataset for a second or two, the dashboard designer screen will be displayed (see Figure 3-24). Press down on the "+" sign in the middle of the screen to add widgets to your dashboard (see Figure 3-25).

Figure 3-24. *Dashboard designer*

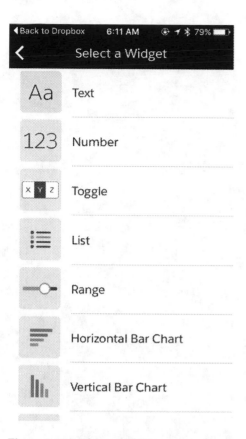

Figure 3-25. *Select a widget type*

2. In the widget selection screen, first select a "Toggle" field and pick the dimension "Year" (see Figure 3-26).

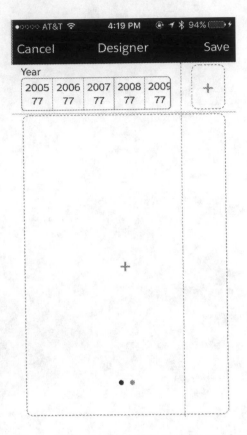

Figure 3-26. *Toggle Field for Year Dimension*

3. Add 3 "Single Number" widgets using the avg, max, and min functions of measure called "Infant Death" (see Figure 3-27).

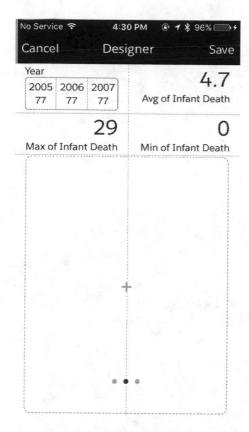

Figure 3-27. *Single number widgets*

4. Continue to add a "V-bar Chart" to display Infant Mortality information grouped by "Community Area Name." Save the dashboard, then view the dashboard, as shown in Figure 3-28. You can also change the view from a bar chart to a donut display using the "view" function, as seen in the graph in Figure 3-29.

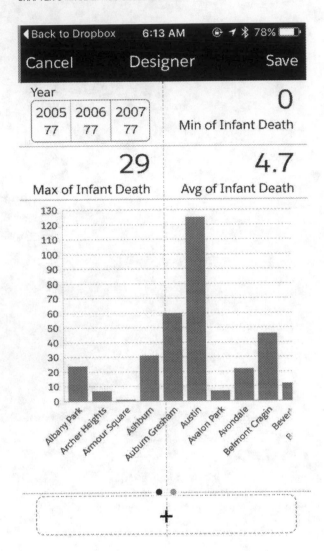

Figure 3-28. *Dashboard with bar chart widget*

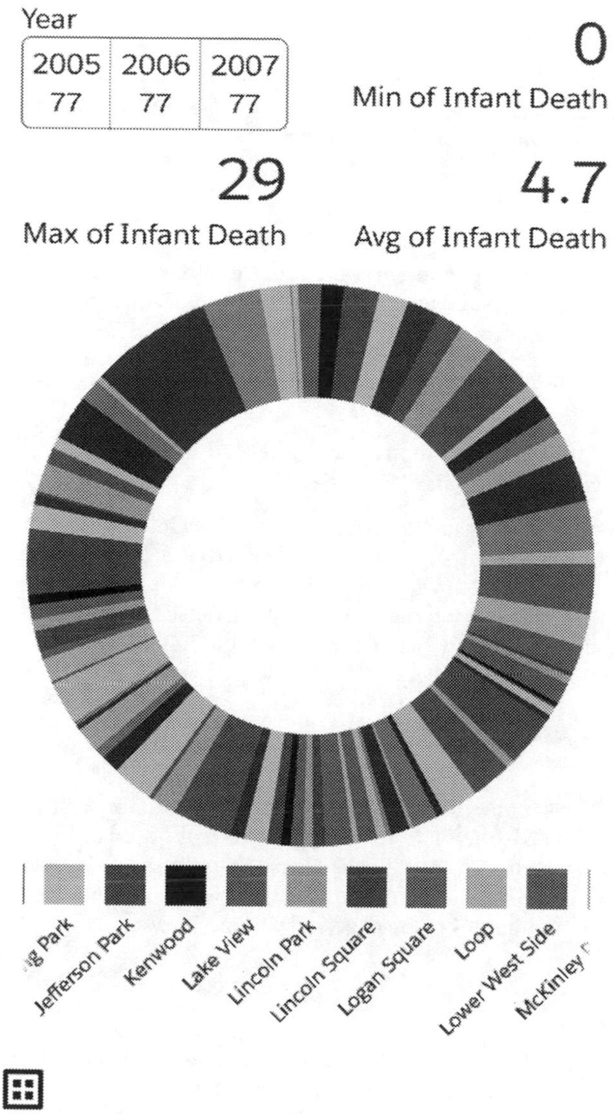
Year
2005 2006 2007
77 77 77
0
Min of Infant Death
29
Max of Infant Death
4.7
Avg of Infant Death
Jefferson Park
Kenwood
Lake View
Lincoln Park
Lincoln Square
Logan Square
Loop
Lower West Side
McKinley

***Figure 3-29.** Explore new view with donut chart*

5. Creating dashboard using mobile devices with Salesforce Analytics is fast and simple. Our quick example above takes less than 15 minutes from data load to dashboard. The interface is intuitive yet powerful for business analysts to explore a dataset and design visualizations, all using a mobile phone.

6. In order to save the dashboard, press "Save" in the upper right corner and provide a name for the dashboard.

Advanced Dashboards

In addition to drag and drop features, Salesforce Analytics Cloud provides rich capabilities for more advanced dashboard design and development. In this section, we'll take a look at these advanced features and how to use them. We'll first start by taking a look at the composition of a Salesforce Analytics dashboard.

Anatomy of a dashboard

A Salesforce Analytics Cloud dashboard is in essence a JSON document containing definitions of the various components of a dashboard and how they are connected together. It is composed of two types of information:

1. System Metadata: It includes information such as UID, Dashboard Name, and Description.

2. Dashboard State: This is where the important information of the dashboard design is stored including Steps, Widgets, and Layouts.

You can configure and modify different aspects of your dashboard through the JSON file. It is recommended, however, that you do not modify any System Metadata through the JSON file.

As described in earlier sections of this chapter, the most convenient method to create and modify a dashboard is through the Dashboard designer either with web interact or your mobile device. However, to create a more advanced dashboard with capabilities such as data join or selection binding, it might be necessary to modify the dashboard definition JSON file.

Dashboard State

The Dashboard State section of dashboard JSON file is under the tag name "state." It contains sub-sections including Steps, Widgets, and Layouts, as we mentioned earlier. The "Steps" portion is composed of all the queries clipped from the lenses through the Dashboard Explorer. Each of these Steps links to a Widget or binds it to another Step through the name field. The Widget section is where all the widgets within the dashboard are defined. The Layout section contains definitions of the page and column layout.

Widgets

The dynamic widget types typically represent each of the query steps. The different widget types include Chart, Raw Data Table, Compare table, Number, Range, List, Date, Toggle, and Global filter.

There are also a number of Static widgets such as Text, Box, YouTube, and Link, which can be configured by the dashboard author. Parameters including size, position, and name can be set as part of the widget properties in the right panel of the Designer/Builder screen.

Steps

Steps contains queries, which have either been clipped from the Explorer, or hand coded SAQL, or through static steps. Selections on steps can be faceted or bound to other steps within the dashboard. We'll cover a selection-binding example in the next section of this chapter. Select mode, start values, is faceted and use global filters can be set as part of step properties.

Layout Canvas

Current implementation of layout canvas in dashboards is fixed in size with absolute positioning on a single page. Future enhancements will include responsive grid, mobile layouts, and templates.

Use of JSON File

Here are the some examples of when you'll be updating the JSON files:

1. Specify a SAQL query, and specify relationships between the query and other steps

2. Populate a selector with a specified list of values instead of from a query

3. Use manual bindings to override the default faceting and manually specify the relationships between the steps

4. Set query limits

5. Specify columns for a values table

For more information about the JSON file, please refer to the "Analytics Cloud Dashboard JSON Reference Guide."

Advanced Dashboard with SAQL

A SAQL script consists of a sequence of statements that are made up of keywords (such as filter, group, and order), identifiers, literals, or special characters. Statements can span multiple lines and must end with a semicolon. SAQL is declarative, which means that you describe what you want to get from your query. Then, the query engine will decide how to efficiently serve it. SAQL is compositional. Every statement has a result, and you can chain statements together. SAQL is influenced by the Pig Latin programming language, however, their implementations differ.

In the next section, we'll show you an example of advanced dashboard development using JSON and SAQL.

Creating Dashboard in Designer

The dataset we are using for this example is called "Consumer Spending", which you can download from www.apress.com/9781484212042 if you'd like to follow along. We'll first create a dashboard using the lens explorer and designer clipping. We then create the following three lenses: Age, Category, and Sum of Value grouped by Item, sorted descending on Sum of Value. We clip them to the designer and add them to 2 list widgets and 1 chart widget. Figure 3-30 depicts the design view of the dashboard. Be sure to save the dashboard so you do not lose your work.

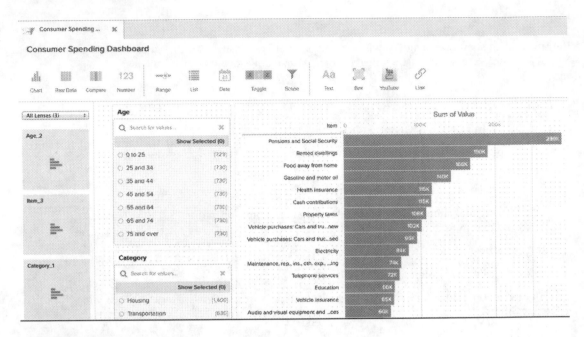

Figure 3-30. *Consumer spending dashboard design view*

Our objective is to only display the top 5 categories based on the age selection. In order to accomplish that, we'll follow these steps to modify the JSON definition of the dashboard.

1. Obtain SAQL Statement: Create a lens with the "Consumer Spending" dataset. Define a measure with "Sum" of "Value" grouped by "Category" and sort with descending order. Create a filter using the "Age" dimension and select 2 random age groups. Click on the "List" icon and select "</> Edit SAQL Query" Note that Salesforce is currently revising the methodology for editing SAQL queries. If you have difficulty in editing the SAQL queries, you should contact Wave support for assistance (see Figure 3-31).

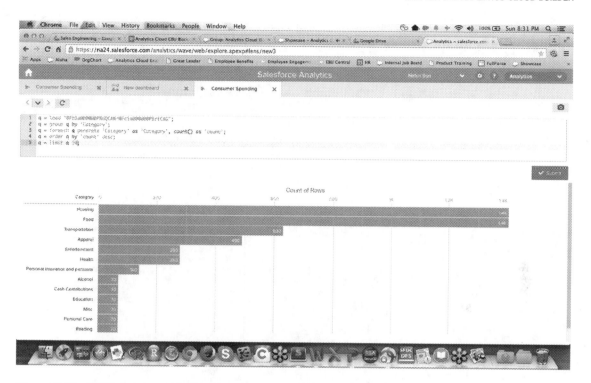

Figure 3-31. *SAQL statement window*

2. Copy and paste the SAQL statement into a text file. Remove the newline characters (or line breaks) and make the statement into one line as follows:

```
q = load "0Fb1a000000PB6QCAW/0Fc1a000000PBrfCAG";q = filter q by 'Age'
== "0 to 25";q = group q by 'Category';q = foreach q generate 'Category'
as 'Category', sum('Value') as 'sum_Value', count() as 'count';q = order
q by 'sum_Value' desc;q = limit q 2000;
```

Save the text file for later use.

3. Navigate to the lens configuration page by replacing in the URL "explore" with "lens" as follows: `https://[domain].salesforce.com/analytics/wave/web/explore.apexp` ➤ `https://[domain].salesforce.com/analytics/wave/web/lens.apexp`

4. Select the dashboard lens and your dashboard JSON file will show up on the text box on the right (see Figure 3-32).

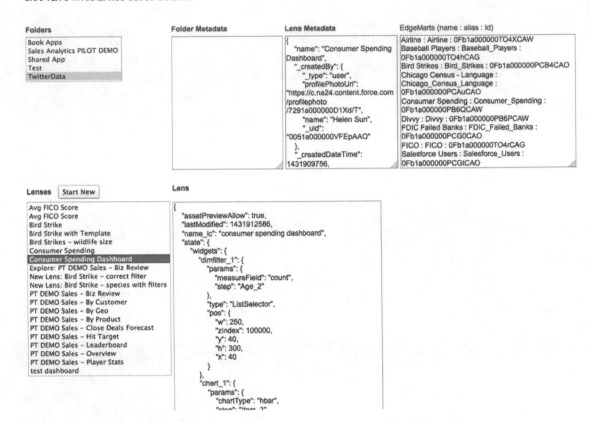

Figure 3-32. *Configuration window*

5. Select the JSON text. Copy and paste it into a JSON editor of your choice. We'll be using Sublime Text. Within the "state" section of the JSON file, locate "steps." Find the step called "Catogory_1" and the "query" section underneath it. Add the following line (the pigql text came from the SAQL statement we copied and pasted into the text file in step 2.

```
"pigql":"q = load \"0Fb1a000000PB6QCAW/0Fc1a000000PBrfCAG\";q = load
"0Fb1a000000PB6QCAW/0Fc1a000000PBrfCAG";q = filter q by 'Age' == "0
to 25";q = group q by 'Category';q = foreach q generate 'Category' as
'Category', sum('Value') as 'sum_Value', count() as 'count';q = order q
by 'sum_Value' desc;q = limit q 2000;",
```

6. Copy and paste the entire JSON file into the lens textbox in the Analytics Cloud screen and click on "Update Lens." Go back to the Analytics home page and refresh the dashboard to ensure the pigql statement is working properly.

7. Go back to the JSON file and update the following:

    a. Change 'Age' == "0 to 25" to 'Age' in {{selection(Age_2)}}

    This is called selecting binding. It basically tells the pigql to use the selection result of the "Age_2" step as the filter for Age in the category selection.

    b. Change limit q 2000 to limit q 5

This is to limit number of result to the top 5 categories of highest amount of consumer spending based on the age group selection.

8. Replace with the new JSON file and click on "Update Lens."

9. Refresh the dashboard and you should be able to see the age group selection will update the category list widget as shown in Figure 3-33.

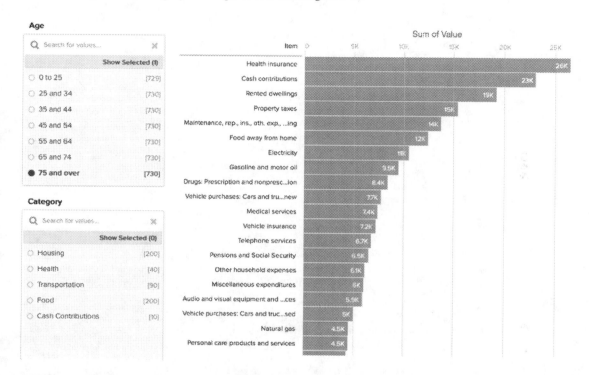

Figure 3-33. *Dynamic selection binding*

Summary

While data is important, without analysis, it is of little value. It's common in this new data era to feel astounded by the explosive amounts of data being collected and shared. Understanding key business drivers and pain points helps business analysts to evaluate what insights are needed. Albert Einstein was on to something when he said we can't always track what we want to count, but that doesn't stop us from constantly exploring new ways to get the data we need.

The success of analytics solution is largely dependent upon human intuition and the ability to ask intelligent questions, both of the business stakeholders and of the data in your analysis approach. Framing a business question properly is essential to avoid flawed analysis and erroneous conclusions.

Salesforce Analytics Cloud is a unique cloud-based analytics tool that gives your knowledge workers the ability to explore data, design effective visualization, and generate insights.

CHAPTER 4

■ ■ ■

Salesforce Analytics Platform

If you know the enemy and know yourself, you need not fear the result of a hundred battles.

—Sun Tzu, *The Art of War*

In Sun Tzu's timeless epic *The Art of War*, the highest value is placed on understanding one's own capabilities and the challenges that lie ahead. The same can be said of a business organization and its analytics software. If you understand your software and your data, you can maximize it to solve your particular problems. In the first three chapters we covered the simplest, user-enabled methods of loading data into the Salesforce Analytics Cloud. Now we look at methods to move data from different sources into the Salesforce Analytics Cloud datasets.

Much of the material presented in this book concerns features of interest to everyday business users, allowing them to create analytics dashboards. This chapter, however, explains some advanced capabilities available with the Salesforce Analytics Cloud, usually the domain of developers and IT professionals. The capabilities described here are relatively new, and certainly some are subject to change; nevertheless, this may be helpful in reviewing your options.

■ **Note**   The information presented is based on what is available at present. It is not an in-depth technical guide; rather, it's a roadmap that helps you survey these technologies. For full technical details, readers should consult the applicable technical documentation and media.

Methods of Data Integration

Analysts at the leading technology research firms regard data integration as a challenge for most analytics software. Yet getting the data into the analytics software, including data discovery products, is essential for using it productively. Luckily, the Salesforce Analytics engine permits data integration through the desktop client or mobile interface, as well as standard user-accessible methods.

There are two methods of data writing to the Salesforce Analytic Cloud and one method for reading the data. The External Data API and Extract Transform Load (ETL) tools are for data writing; the Wave REST API is for reading the data. Each of these methods serves a different need, so it is important to understand their features before deciding which you might use. Figure 4-1 presents an overview of the methods.

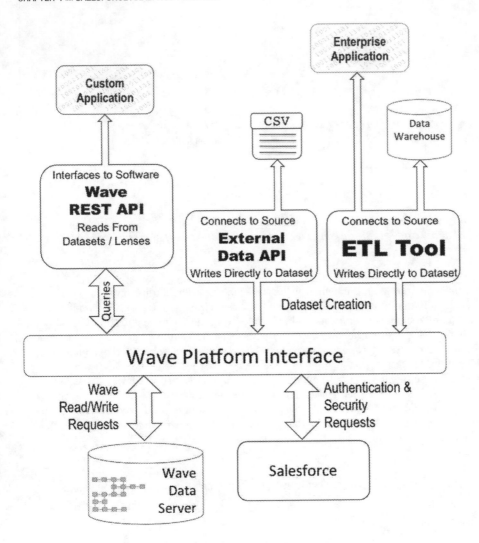

Figure 4-1. *Data integration methods for the Salesforce Analytics Cloud*

- **The External Data API**. The External Data API is used to create datasets. It is the choice for companies that want to load large amounts of data without using enterprise software, like ETL tools. For example, this is likely the approach for companies who develop particular products; they have their custom software-development capability, with software developers on staff who are familiar with REST API development in general.

- **ETL Tools**. Extract Transform Load (ETL) tools make data integration easier with graphic interfaces, scheduling capability, and support for connection to nearly any type of data source. They usually have pre-built connectors to enterprise software platforms like SAP or NetSuite, which makes data access easier. The upside is their short development time; however, ETL tools can be costly. Purchasing an ETL tool solely to integrate data with the Salesforce Analytics Cloud would be difficult to justify. Organizations should examine their Salesforce partner ETL tools to determine if they have native support for the Salesforce Analytics Cloud.

- **The Wave REST API**. The Wave REST API is used for reading data from the Salesforce Analytics Cloud (versus obtaining data, as in the case of ETL Tools and the External Data API). Companies developing products that use the Salesforce Analytics Cloud would then use the Wave REST API. These products could be mobile applications or desktop computer products that are BI capable. Companies with custom software development capability can use the Wave REST API to build applications that retrieve data from the Salesforce Analytics Cloud.

Now, let's take a closer look at each of these.

External Data API

The External Data API provides the capability of integrating external data into the Salesforce Analytics Cloud. The external data is loaded directly into datasets, and is then available for queries or for mobile or desktop use of the Salesforce Analytics Cloud. The following steps, shown in Figure 4-2, are followed so as to use the External Data API.

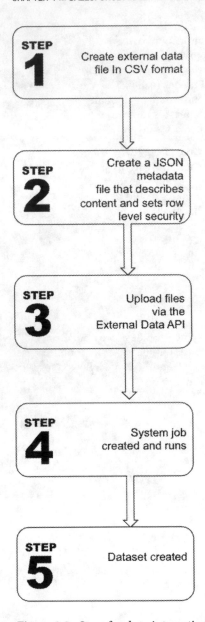

STEP 1 Create external data file In CSV format

STEP 2 Create a JSON metadata file that describes content and sets row level security

STEP 3 Upload files via the External Data API

STEP 4 System job created and runs

STEP 5 Dataset created

Figure 4-2. Steps for data integration using External Data API

Step 1. Create .CSV File

All data is put into .csv format and written to a file to load into the Salesforce Analytics Cloud using the External Data API, regardless of the source. As a programming task, this is generally easy, but care must be taken to ensure the file created is not too large. (See "Restrictions on Use" that follows.) Care also must be taken to use quoted identifiers if the source has a comma or CR/LF. Any quotes in a value surrounded by quoted identifiers need to be escaped by another set of quotes; for example, "Don't ""quote"" me."

Step 2. Create JSON Metadata

The JSON metadata file describes the data so that when each row is loaded, the Salesforce Analytics Cloud is able to determine the data type for each column. To create this file, you identify as a date, number, or string each of the fields of the .csv file created in step 1. This file also determines what, if any, security is applied to each row. The Salesforce Analytic Cloud maintains a document specifically to record this metadata, so developers should refer to this document to fully understand the JSON format.

Step 3. Upload Files

This step is twofold. The first part is to connect to Salesforce. There are a variety of methods for authenticating into Salesforce and any will suffice. According to Salesforce, the venerable SOAP-based authentication methods or the newer REST-based can be used to establish connectivity.

The second part involves uploading the files by using an object known as the InsightsExternalData object. Salesforce requires that files larger than 10MB be broken into 10MB "chunks," then uploaded with the InsightsExternalData object.

Step 4. System Job Is Created and Run

This job is created automatically after the uploading is completed; it does not need to be initiated by the developer. The system job-processes the .csv file data and the JSON metadata.

Step 5. Dataset Is Created

The dataset creation occurs as a result of step 4, and thus is not initiated by the developer, either. Once the dataset is created, it is ready for use in the Salesforce Analytics Cloud.

Restrictions on Use

Certain restrictions are placed on the External Data API, based on information current as of this writing and they are subject to change. If you need to extend your use of the External Data API, contact Salesforce. The restrictions are as follows:

1. A maximum of 50 files per day can be uploaded, with all external data uploads occurring in a rolling 24-hour period.

2. Each file can have a maximum file size of 40G.

3. The maximum number of characters in a field is 32K.

4. For each record, the maximum number of fields is 5K.

5. The maximum number of characters for all fields in a record is 400K.

The first two limits are the most restrictive, especially item 1. The others are not likely to be of concern in most circumstances.

Supporting Documents

Salesforce provides a number of documents for developers to review so as to implement the External Data API. These documents provide a high level of detail and are as follows:

Analytics Cloud External Data API Developer's Guide. Describes the overall process and provides some code examples in the "C" programming language. Includes information on the InsightsExternalData object.

Analytics Cloud External Data Format Reference. Describes the JSON format needed, discussed in step 2.

Security Implementation Guide for Analytics Cloud. Explanation of the various modes of security for the Salesforce Analytics Cloud. A long document that is somewhat nuanced and many details shown are more relevant to Salesforce data loaded in the Salesforce Analytics Cloud.

Extract Transform Load Tools

The Extract Transform Load (ETL) tools have seen widespread use in information technology and are one of the most commonly used classes of IT software. Many companies provide ETL tools, and most are feature-rich and capable of connecting to nearly any type of data source, including back-office enterprise software, relational databases, flat files, and data provided via APIs. ETL tools also are able to achieve data transformation without needing software developers. Figure 4-3 shows the general flow when an ETL tool is used with the Salesforce Analytics Cloud.

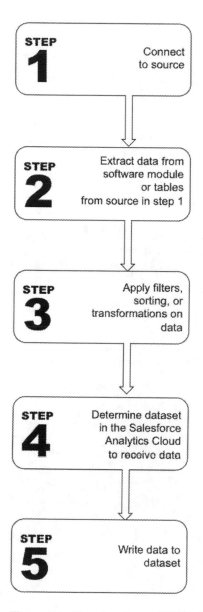

STEP 1 Connect to source

STEP 2 Extract data from software module or tables from source in step 1

STEP 3 Apply filters, sorting, or transformations on data

STEP 4 Determine dataset in the Salesforce Analytics Cloud to receive data

STEP 5 Write data to dataset

Figure 4-3. *Steps in using an ETL tool to write data to the Salesforce Analytics Cloud*

Configuring the ETL software is a relatively simple task for most users. Let's discuss a few details.

Step 1. Connect to Source

Most ETL packages boast connectivity to many hundreds of types of data sources. This step is to connect to one of those sources, and usually all that is needed is the hostname for the source, username, and password.

Step 2. Extract Data

The key to success in this step is having a developer or analyst who understands the source data and knows which tables or other entities to use. For this step to succeed, the step 1 username must have access or security privileges for the source tables or entities.

Step 3. Sort, Filter, and Transform

Most ETL packages provide graphic means to map source data to target columns, transform the data, and filter out ranges of values that are not needed. For the Salesforce Analytics Cloud, this is where you ensure the data types for each column are correct and you select the column names in the dataset.

Step 4. Determine the Dataset

You select the dataset in the Salesforce Analytics Cloud that is to receive the data. If the dataset does not exist, it will be created. In this step, you specify the write method for the data, which could include deleting existing data and then writing data or appending to an existing dataset.

Step 5. Write the Dataset

You write the data to the Salesforce Analytics Cloud. But before you do so, you authenticate into Salesforce. When the ETL tool has been authenticated, the ETL tool writes directly to the Salesforce Analytics Cloud. This step assumes that you are using an ETL tool with native support for the Salesforce Analytics Cloud. To ensure native support, select from one of the ETL vendors that supports the Salesforce Analytics Cloud. One of the easiest ways to find these vendors is on the dataset creation page of the Salesforce Analytics Cloud; this is shown in Figure 4-4.

Select a Data Source

Salesforce   CSV   Informatica Rev

Additional Partners

Informatica   Mulesoft   Jitterbit   Boomi   Snaplogic   IBM   Talend

Figure 4-4. *Partners listing on dataset creation page*

Of the companies shown in Figure 4-4, Informatica, Mulesoft, Jitterbit, Dell Boomi, Snaplogic, and Talend all have a strong ETL product line with a focus on this area of technology. IBM has a number of products that integrate with the Salesforce Analytics Cloud, above and beyond ETL tools.

One of the advantages of the Salesforce Analytics Cloud is that Salesforce ensures its products are partnered with the products of other IT companies. Many of these partners have white papers, demo videos, and interactive websites that demonstrate how their products integrate with the Salesforce Analytics Cloud.

Wave REST API

As mentioned earlier, the Wave REST API is a tool for retrieving data from the Salesforce Analytics Cloud. As of this writing, the Wave REST API is a pilot project of Salesforce, not generally available to the public. Those interested in participating in the Wave REST API pilot program should contact Salesforce.

You might be wondering about the acronym REST. It stands for "representational state transfer" and is a distributed computing standard method for exposing APIs on the World Wide Web. REST is gradually replacing an older distributed computing method known as SOAP.

Conclusion

This chapter presented two technologies for moving data from different sources outside of Salesforce into the Salesforce Analytics Cloud datasets. The first technology we looked at was the External Data API, primarily targeted at customer solution development. The second technology was the ETL tools that have native support for the Salesforce Analytics Cloud. ETL tools are the easiest path to getting your data into the Salesforce Analytics Cloud, but they require investment. Also, ETL tools require expertise to be used correctly, and this is also a consideration.

We also looked at a technology for retrieving data from the Salesforce Analytics Cloud, the Wave REST API. Though not currently available to the general public, organizations can apply to participate in a pilot program.

Business Analytics Solutions Using the Salesforce Analytics Cloud

■ ■ ■

CHAPTER 5

Critical Decision Making and the Salesforce Analytics Cloud

Without data, anyone who does anything is free to claim success.

—Angus Deaton, *The Great Escape*

In the preface to his 2015 book *The Great Escape: Health, Wealth, and the Origins of Inequality*, Nobel Prize–winning economist Angus Deaton notes that claiming success in the absence of supporting data is an all too common occurrence in our world today, and it often causes a lack of confidence in the agencies and institutions charged with maintaining and protecting the welfare of our society. To support the conclusions and statements in his book, Deaton always provides the data, the sources of that data, and a view of how credible (or incredible) those sources are.

Using data to support decisions and reach conclusions is the foundation for critical decision making. Companies that make better, faster decisions—and act on them effectively—will almost always outpace their competitors. For making big, high-value choices, this fact is obvious. The critical decisions likely include introducing a new product or moving a manufacturing base to Asia, since these choices involve sizable resources and significant risk.

Less obvious are decisions made week in and week out that are equally important but less dramatic. These types of decisions are most often operational, and they are made and executed by those on or near the frontline. The net effect of these equally important decisions can amount to spending or saving thousands or even millions of dollars. Yet we are in a data-rich era of information technology, in which we aim to capture as much information as possible and utilize analytics to facilitate this data-driven decision making. How do we meet this challenge?

With so many decisions to be made, and a shortage of data scientists to perform the necessary analyses, there's a trend toward using data-discovery products that enable everyday users—mere mortals—to perform data analysis. In this chapter, we focus on a use case to demonstrate how such tools can be used to make many of these day-to-day decisions. Our use case is a company that both manufactures glass itself and makes various products from that glass.

Critical Decision Making and Cognitive Bias

Before we jump into the use case, though, let's examine the nature of critical decision making and consider why so many of us are so bad at it. In approaching the topic of critical decision making, thought-leaders point out that the biggest barrier to making the right or correct decision is bias. As individual decision makers we are all subject to *cognitive bias*—assumptions that we hold that become mental modes of action impeding us from making decisions in a rational manner. Cognitive bias takes many forms; here are a few examples.

- **Recency Bias** This bias is our tendency to be affected disproportionately by our most recent experiences. For example, many people believe that the financial crisis that occurred in 2007 is the greatest failure in the history of our banking system; yet the savings and loan crisis of the late 1980s was a far more costly event for the FDIC. This fact is easily verified by examining the publicly available data from the FDIC.

- **Sunk Cost Bias** This bias stems from our tendency to throw good money after bad. Companies will often invest in technologies that turn out to be faulty, and then expend a disproportionate amount of human capital to make the technologies work.

- **Overconfidence Bias** A feeling of overconfidence characterizes those who experience success through luck or unusual circumstances, without having faced adversity. This causes them to neglect due diligence and risk assessment in making their decisions. For instance, IBM once so dominated the computer industry that it was inconceivable the company would ever relinquish its position. When IBM created its personal computer, they based it on an open architecture that could be copied by anyone, they used a microprocessor supplied by Intel, and they installed an operating system supplied by Microsoft. IBM believed their market dominance would prevent others from competing, but in a short time Compaq produced the first IBM PC–compatible machine, or clone. IBM's overconfidence helped Microsoft and Intel to ultimately become two of the largest technology companies in the PC age. In speaking about IBMs epic decision to make an open-architecture PC, Microsoft founder Bill Gates described success as a menace, something that fools smart people into believing they can't lose.

Data-discovery products like the Salesforce Analytics Cloud enable critical decision making by empowering us to use data to the greatest extent possible, thereby avoiding bias. These products eliminate factors that cause us to make errors in our decision making and help us avoid pitfalls like cognitive bias. In this chapter's use case, we see how such a tool can be used to better manage manufacturing operations and evaluate personnel performance at many levels.

The Use Case Manufacturer

Our manufacturing example has a number of distinct data domains, and we examine two of them in some detail. The first domain we cover relates to the instrument and control data associated with monitoring and controlling production processes. The second domain concerns the performance of manufacturing facilities, both at a facility level and for the entire corporation. We feature these two different domains to illustrate how the Salesforce Analytics Cloud can easily handle any data, from the plant floor to the boardroom.

As some readers may not be familiar with manufacturing processes, or the instrument and control data associated with typical manufacturing, a little background information is in order. For instance, you may be familiar with the much-hyped term Internet of Things, or IoT. This refers to the vast array of devices that have Ethernet connectivity, including everything from air conditioners to aircraft. In making the case for adoption of technologies associated with Big Data, vendors and technical evangelists point out that IoT produces data faster than at any other time in history. Those involved in manufacturing already probably have first-hand experience with this rate of data production, as manufacturing facilities have been amassing such data for decades in their relational databases.

However, to introduce this domain, let's look at the process of glass manufacturing, focusing on the instrument and control data involved. Figure 5-1 is a historical overview of the process. Eventually, we will employ this background information to cover the types of glass manufacturing facilities and the operational data associated with them, as well as how the Salesforce Analytics Cloud operates in these two domains to provide improved bases for decision making.

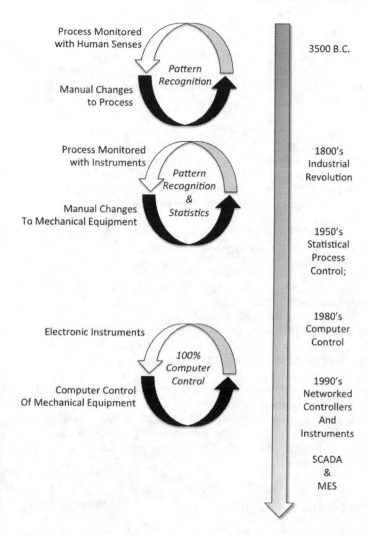

Figure 5-1. *A brief history of glass manufacturing data and control*

Early Glass Making

Glass was made in ancient Egypt and Mesopotamia as early as 3500 BCE, and porcelain was made in China as early as 1600 BCE. In these times, there were no machines; the process involved melting and shaping the silica by hand, with the glass maker regulating the intensity of the heat and controlling the flow of air. Early glass making relied on the skill of that craftsman to monitor—skills that were acquired over many years of apprenticeship. These craftsmen relied on their ability to recognize patterns in the material and make decisions on an intuitive level. Art glass is still produced in this manner today, but the bulk of our commercial glass production is manufactured industrially.

Early Instrumentation and Increased Statistical Process Control

Over the centuries, reliance on pattern recognition gave way to modern manufacturing processes in all types of production, not just glass making. Instruments were used to measure basic physical properties of the materials during the process, like temperature, pressure, and airflow, allowing factory workers to manually change process inputs with simple on/off devices such as motors, or by opening or closing a value to control temperature.

By the 1950s, physical measurements from instruments used in manufacturing were combined with statistical analysis, producing systems of monitoring and thereby imposing more control of product quality. The best known example of this innovation is Statistical Process Control, or SPC, pioneered by W. Edwards Deming in postwar Japan. By the 1980s, SPC was adopted by U.S. manufacturers as well. It represents one of the most important manufacturing changes of the twentieth century, ushering in a new era of quality in manufacturing. SPC is also an early excellent example of how data can be used to drive decision making.

Automatic Control via Computer Technology

Computer technology began making an impact on the control of manufacturing processes in the 1980s, in several different areas. As a result, these technologies enabled more precise control of manufacturing processes. Instrumentation, when combined with basic control devices such as solenoids (a type of magnetic on/off switch) or more sophisticated control devices (like variable-flow control valves) enabled "closed loop control" using small microprocessor-based controllers. Here, the term "loop" refers to the loop formed by the inputs to and outputs from a controller, forming a circle with the controller at one end and the process equipment at the other. These controllers allowed unprecedented control over manufacturing processes.

Programmable controllers were introduced in the 1980s, providing a flexible, easy-to-program platform for control of manufacturing processes. These programmable controllers were initially designed to offer a computer-based method of replicating the logic diagrams used by engineers and electricians to perform discrete control, whereby there are only digital inputs and outputs in a manufacturing process. Later versions of programmable controllers replicated the function of loop controllers but were also capable of controlling systems with hundreds of inputs and outputs.

Data Networks Offer Increased Integration

In the 1990s, there emerged networks for instrumentation as a way to configure and monitor the instruments. These instrumentation networks also simplified the wiring of the instruments, requiring only a single data communications cable to be run among all the instruments on a production line. The instruments could not only indicate a physical property but also report on their "health" and allow operational parameters of the devices to be changed. For example, a photoelectric sensor often needs to be adjusted to ensure it is properly sensing objects as they pass in front of it. Now, adjustments could be made to that photoelectric sensor using the instrument data network.

Electric motors are one of the most critical elements of a manufacturing process, and motor controllers are usually called "drives." (We will discuss drives later in this chapter.) Device networks are also used for these drives, allowing them to be configured across the network and providing complete operational data, which includes speed of rotation, electric current, and if and when a motor is going to fail.

The data from instrumentation and programmable controllers has been collected and stored in databases for over 20 years, utilizing supervisory systems known as Supervisory Control and Data Acquisition (SCADA) systems and in Manufacturing Execution Systems (MES). Figure 5-2 shows how SCADA and MES systems are networked with the controllers and instrumentation just discussed.

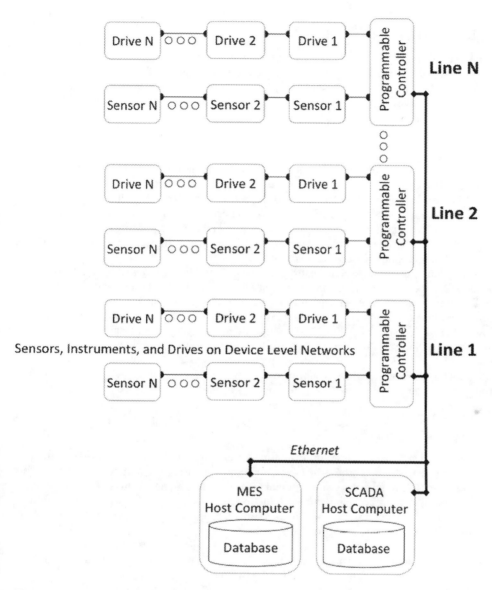

Figure 5-2. *SCADA and MES network*

SCADA systems acquire and store instrumentation and controller data for later review to determine the root cause of any problems or the timing of a failure. Both SCADA and MES systems acquire data that enables them to show the performance of manufacturing processes, track product lots, and record raw material consumption.

Company Structure and Facilities

Let's examine some manufacturing companies and the types of facilities usually found in these companies. Organizations that are involved in manufacturing often have many facilities that contain major manufacturing processes. For example, the glass company in our use case has three types of facilities: float glass plants, glass fabrication plants, and automotive encapsulation facilities. Let's examine each of these.

Float Glass Plants

Float glass plants are facilities involved in the manufacture of glass from raw materials. These facilities melt silica sand and soda ash in a large furnace to produce a massive, continuous ribbon of glass that is cut into rectangular pieces. It is then shipped to other facilities to make things like automotive windows and glass windows for homes and buildings. These float glass facilities usually have one or two furnace lines that are hundreds of yards long. Float glass plants are so named because of the manufacturing process used to produce the glass. In this process, the molten glass is drawn out of the furnace into a bath of molten tin to cool, thereby ensuring that both sides of the glass are clear and flat.

A float glass plant is many times larger than a fabrication facility, and it consumes substantial amounts of natural gas, used to melt the raw materials. The plant must run continuously 24 hours per day so as to maintain the stability of the process. When an equipment failure occurs on a production line, the glass production continues and the glass is crushed and refed into the furnace until the repairs are completed. The uptime metric here is the percentage of time the line is producing *usable* glass. An equipment outage drives this percentage down, but so do other events, such as product changeovers. That is, sometimes there has to be a change in the thickness or tint of the glass being produced. Making these production changes can destabilize the line for hours or even days, resulting in downtime and refed glass that is too brittle to cut. Limiting the number of changeovers thus maximizes the facility's uptime.

Glass Fabrication Plants

Some of the glass fabrication facilities in our example manufacturer make automotive windows by cutting a sheet of glass into particular shapes, smoothing the edges, and bending the glass to match the contour of the automobile model for which it is intended. The operational focus is vastly different from the float glass plant. Instead of one major operation, there are many small production lines, each of which often performs a single task. An equipment failure on one of these production lines can affect uptime, not only for the line with the equipment failure but also for the overall plant output.

Fabrication facilities must be cognizant of product quality, as the glass that goes into automobiles must be free of defects. In the float glass plants, the quality issues are obvious—usually bubbles or visible defects that are easily detected with laser inspection; the defective pieces are scrapped immediately. In the fabrication facility, however, quality issues can be harder to detect. They are usually found only after production of a piece of automotive glass has been completed. If a defective piece of automotive glass reaches a customer, there are chargebacks to the facility and possible loss of quality reputation, which ultimately results in loss of that customer.

Automotive Encapsulation Facilities

The third facility type for our example manufacturer has a simple operation: encapsulating the automotive glass in a polymer for strength and ease of installation on an automobile assembly line. We don't cover this type of facility in this chapter.

The Organization of the Company's Plants

Figure 5-3 shows the organizational structure of our use case glass company.

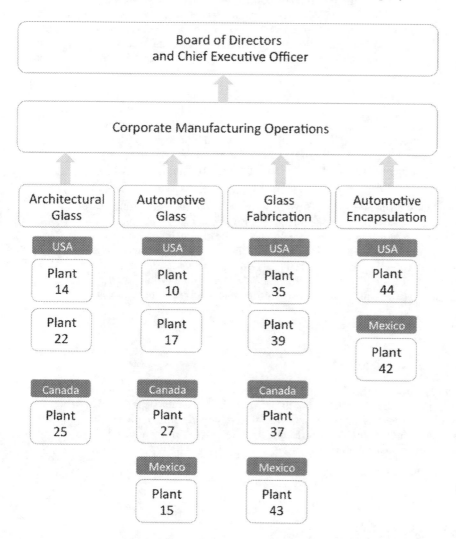

Figure 5-3. *Organizational structure of the glass company*

As Figure 5-3 shows, there are seven float glass plants, producing glass for automotive and architectural uses. Automative glass is tinted for use in automobiles, and some glass has properties that block ultraviolet light to protect automotive interiors. This glass is tinted for use in automobiles, and some glass has properties that block ultraviolet light to protect automotive interiors. There are also four glass fabrication plants and two automotive encapsulation plants.

In the sections that follow, we examine the data from these facilities and use the Salesforce Analytics Cloud to create dashboards that provide useful data visualizations. Recall from Chapter 1 that there are two basic types of analytics enabled by the Salesforce Analytics Cloud: descriptive analytics (answering the question "What happened?") and diagnostic analytics (answering the question "Why did it happen?"). Let's look at some real data and learn how the descriptive and prescriptive analytics can be performed.

Key Performance Indicators

In our use case, there is a leadership team focused on management of all manufacturing facilities. This team consists of the plant management at each facility and the managers at the company's headquarters. The team focuses on operations and planning, and it monitors the facilities on a daily basis, making critical decisions to maximize performance and profitability, and then communicating the results. The monitoring is based on data that is categorized as *key performance indicators* (KPIs), among which are throughput, yield, and uptime.

- **Throughput:** The throughput KPI is the number of parts or amount of material that passes through a production line. Production lines often have bottlenecks, and making improvements to avoid these bottlenecks can be profitable if the cost of instituting them is low enough. If the equipment on a production line experiences frequent downtime, the result is decreased throughput, obviously. For any production line, the capability with regard to throughput is well understood, based on design and operational history.

- **Yield:** The yield KPI is the percentage of usable product made. A yield of 100 percent on most production lines is impossible; manufacturing processes always produce some scrap product. At the end of a production line is the quality inspection, done by machines or humans. For example, a production line producing automotive windows will end with inspection for visual problems, especially scratches. Any window with a scratch must be discarded, thereby decreasing the yield of that production line. To calculate the yield, we perform the following computation:

    ```
    Yield % = number of quality parts produced / throughput.
    ```

- The percentage of product that is discarded due to quality problems is sometimes referred to as the *scrap rate*.

- **Uptime:** Ideally, the equipment on a production line never stops operating, but of course this is not possible. Invariably, equipment does fail and must be repaired. Manufacturing facilities have maintenance personnel charged with repairing equipment that has failed, as well as performing preventative maintenance on equipment to lessen the probability of failure.

Now, let's a look at a dashboard created in the Salesforce Analytics Cloud to report these throughput, yield, and uptime parameters.

Facility-Level Reporting

Plant 35, shown in Figure 5-3, is a glass fabrication facility that uses the glass from the float glass plants to produce windows for automobiles. The plant operates continuously, and a production management team is responsible for monitoring performance. There are three shifts in a 24-hour period, with the first shift starting at 8:00 AM, second at 4:00 PM, and third at 12:00 midnight.

There are four production lines running. A shift foreman who is part of the production management team is the frontline manager who makes critical, minute-to-minute decisions that ensure all four lines are running optimally. The SCADA system performs extensive data acquisition on the programmable controllers that operate the four production lines. With this information, SCADA is able to report the yield, throughput, and uptime for each line. On any day, the production management team uses a dashboard in the Salesforce Analytics Cloud to see what happened during the previous three shifts. A screenshot from the dashboard is shown in Figure 5-4.

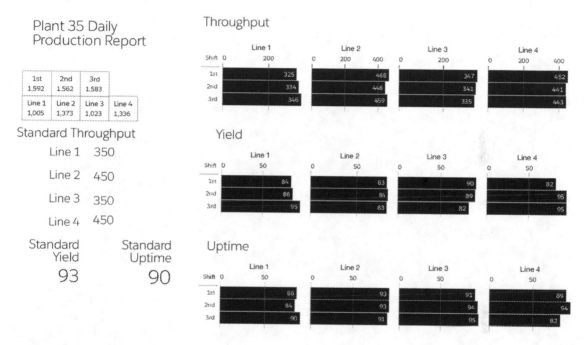

Figure 5-4. *Daily Production Report for Plant 35*

Figures 5-5 and 5-6 show more readable views of the left and right sides, respectively of the Figure 5-4 dashboard.

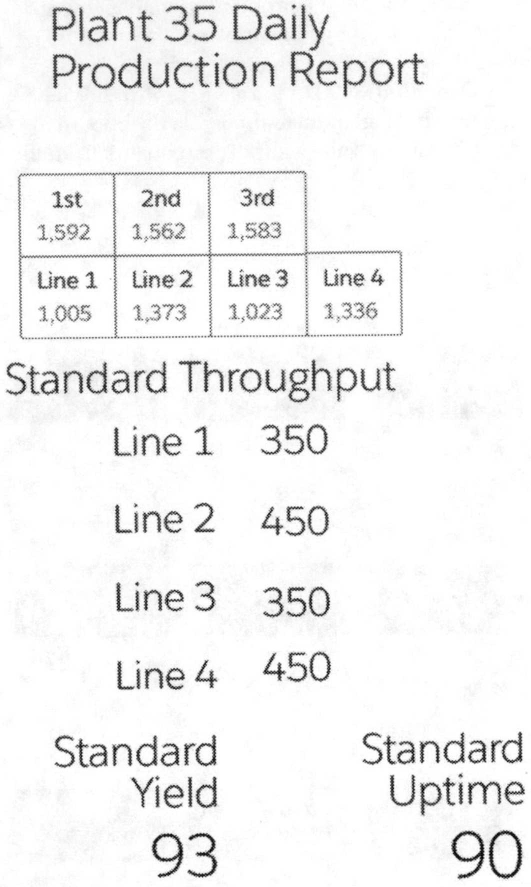

Plant 35 Daily Production Report

1st	2nd	3rd	
1,592	1,562	1,583	

Line 1	Line 2	Line 3	Line 4
1,005	1,373	1,023	1,336

Standard Throughput

Line 1	350
Line 2	450
Line 3	350
Line 4	450

Standard Yield	Standard Uptime
93	90

Figure 5-5. *Left side of Daily Production Report for Plant 35*

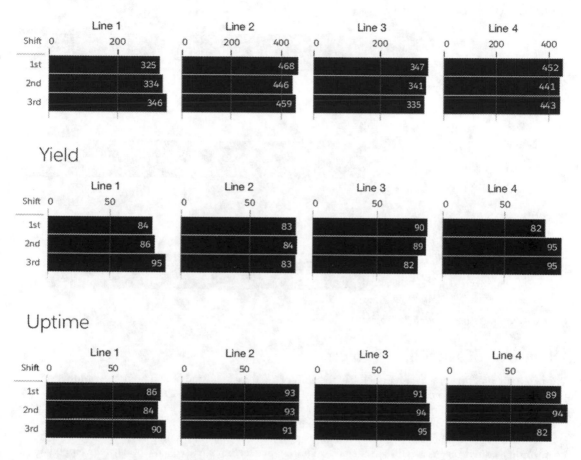

Figure 5-6. Right side of Daily Production Report for Plant 35

At this plant, lines 1 and 3 are identical, as are lines 2 and 4. Therefore, the production reporting for lines 1 and 3 should be close to identical if both lines are running at optimum. The dashboard shows "standard" numbers for the yield, throughput, and uptime KPIs; these are minimum performance numbers that the production lines should be able to achieve every day. However, Figure 5-6 shows that line 1 had difficulties during first and second shifts.

The dashboard has toggle widgets so the user can select the production line for closer viewing. Since line 1 had the problems, we press the line 1 toggle widget; the result is shown in Figure 5-7.

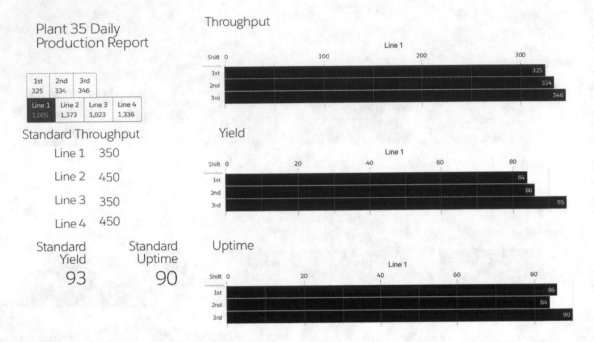

Figure 5-7. *Line 1 view, selected using toggle widget*

Diagnosis of Machine Problem

The problem affecting line 1 was corrected at the start of the third shift, and at that point the production performance returned to normal. During the course of those two earlier shifts, though, operators attempted to correct the problem themselves, but were not successful. The shift foreman for the third shift noticed the downward trend on the dashboard and called in maintenance personnel.

A maintenance technician determined that the problem was an abnormally low lubricant level in a gearbox on a conveyor. (As we will see later, the maintenance technician used a dashboard developed in Wave Analytics to zero in on the problem.) By way of explanation, know that the gearbox is attached to a motor, which is in turn connected to a drive, which controls its speed. The drive is connected to a device-level network. Diagnostic information is collected from the drive by a programmable controller, with data ultimately stored in a SCADA system. For each conveyor, there is a button that resets the control logic in the programmable controller and clears any drive faults. Figure 5-8 depicts these components for one conveyor on line 1.

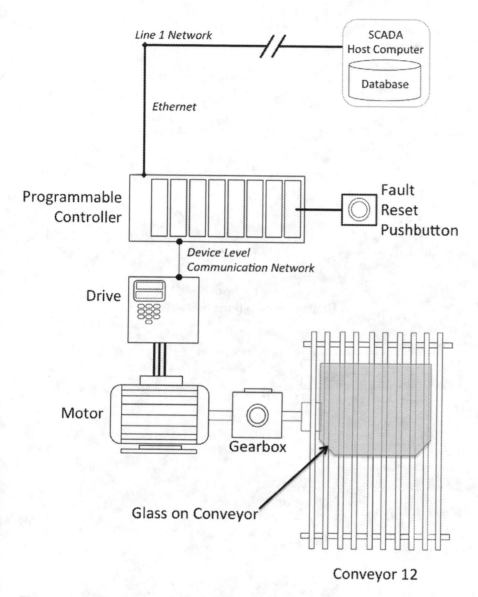

Figure 5-8. *Mechanical and control equipment for conveyor on line 1*

Operators tend to use the reset button to clear faults quickly, and they do not always determine the reason a conveyor has stopped. Faults are often attributed, therefore, to an incorrect cause that may not have existed. Yet tracking such faults is critical to improving performance; refining the maintenance practices can help address such recurring problems. In the case of the drive fault that occurred on line 1 because of a low gearbox lubricant level, preventive maintenance should include checking these lubricant levels.

However, in this instance, the maintenance worker was able to diagnose this problem with data collected from the line 1 drives, made available in the dashboard. Here's how: An average reading of electric current is maintained for each drive, and it is based on empirically collected data gathered over the last three months. The average current for each shift is also calculated by the SCADA system, as is the highest and lowest current readings. Figure 5-9 depicts the flow for data collected for each conveyor.

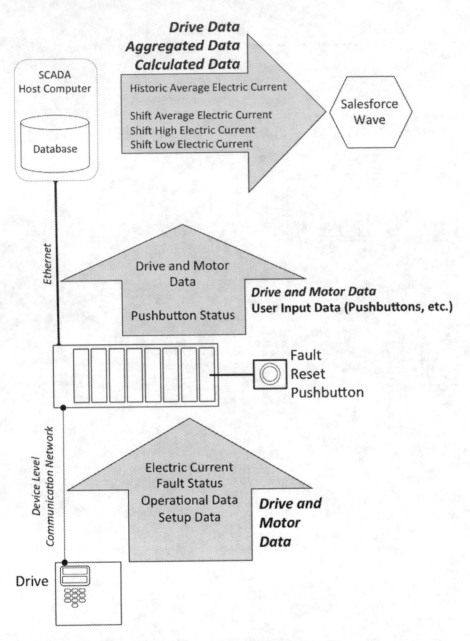

Figure 5-9. *Data flow for conveyor operational monitoring*

The collected electrical data is incorporated into a dashboard shown in Figure 5-10. This dashboard reveals all of the data on electric current collected for all three shifts. The dashboard thus readily identifies any drive with overly high electrical current conditions. A bubble chart pinpoints any drives having consistently higher current than normal. (By way of explanation, the delta high current is the difference between the average current for the drive and the highest current recorded for a shift.) The bubbles on the left indicate normally running drives; the bubbles on the right show an anomaly and should be investigated.

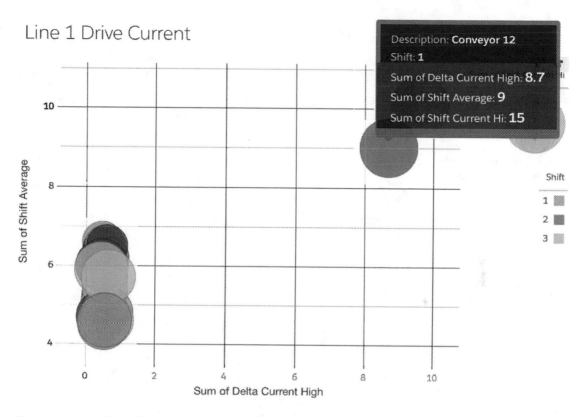

Figure 5-10. *Dashboard for line 1, shift 1 current use*

In this case, the bubble chart provided data for the three shifts, as shown in Figure 5-10. The maintenance technician saw the two bubbles on the right and selected to view additional information associated with them. Both of the bubbles show high current readings for conveyor 12, which led that maintenance technician to investigate the mechanical system associated with conveyor 12, and ultimately to find the low gearbox lubrication level.

Eliminating Cognitive Bias with Data

This use case shows how data can be used to thwart cognitive bias in resolving problems of machine failure. Production workers have a strong incentive to keep their lines running, so they tend to clear the faults quickly and "guess" why a failure occurred. Their guesses, though, are often based on most recent experience, perhaps on other production lines, and thus are a good example of the recency bias mentioned earlier. Understandably, plant management is quick to defend this practice because of its desire to keep the production lines running, but ultimately the approach is detrimental to performance. In this example, data was used to find the true cause of the problem.

Corporate-Level Reporting

Now let's look at some examples involving corporate-level data use. As shown in Figure 5-3, there is a corporate hierarchy in our glass company at both the facility level and corporate headquarters. Turnover in these leadership positions is normal, so having a quick reference for managers who are "ramping up" makes these transitions easier. Rather that put this information into a published manual, the glass company has a dashboard that presents a quick summary of the float glass manufacturing facilities, based on the tonnage of glass produced per day.

What is compelling about this summary is its versatility. On the desktop client, there is a dashboard that allows refinement based on country, glass product type, and plant number. Figure 5-11 shows this desktop web browser dashboard.

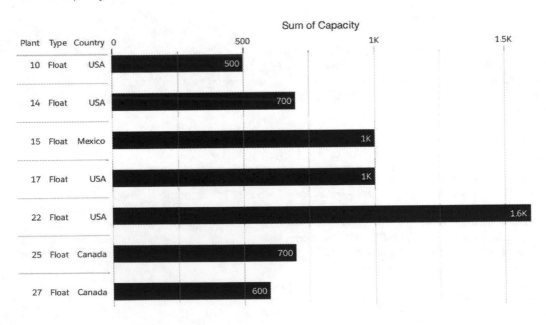

Figure 5-11. *Dashboard for float glass capacity*

When a manager selects USA as the country, the dashboard changes to the one shown in Figure 5-12.

Float Glass Capacity Dashboard

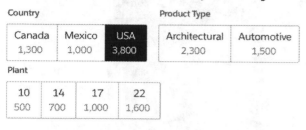

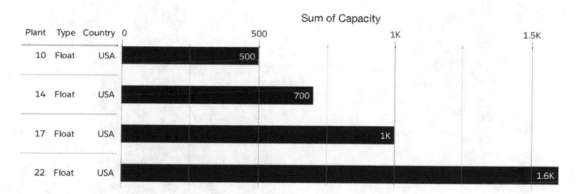

Figure 5-12. *Dashboard for USA float glass capacity*

This dashboard is also available on the Apple iPhone and the Apple Watch, as shown in Figure 5-13.

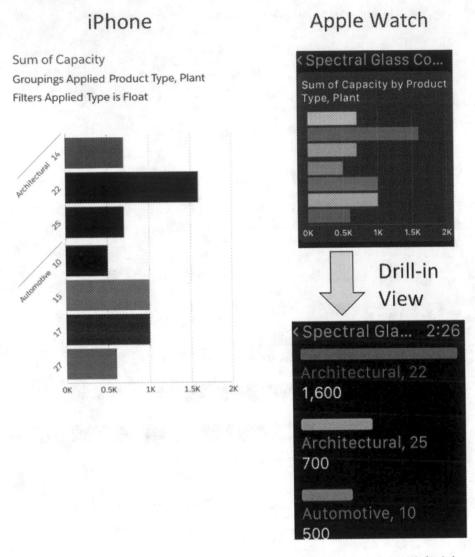

Figure 5-13. *Dashboard for float glass capacity, on iPhone (left) and Apple Watch (right)*

This simple dashboard showing production capacity can be created from a dataset based on an Excel spreadsheet, and it can be done in minutes. This speed makes the Salesforce Analytics Cloud the most expeditious way to make valuable information available, with a user interface that allows the data to be refined easily on either a desktop or mobile device. But let's look at some examples of this.

Assessing Plant Manager Performance

Within most major corporations, the plant managers are in charge of the manufacturing facilities, and corporate leadership is constantly assessing the performance of those plant managers. The KPIs for an entire year are typically used to assess their performance. The Salesforce Analytics Cloud makes this task easy.

For example, the performance numbers for yield, uptime, and throughput for of our glass company's float glass facilities are collected into one dashboard, shown in Figure 5-11. This data is obtained by using the *calendar heat map* widget, a powerful visualization tool that allows considerable data to be viewed at one glance. On this dashboard, the yield, uptime, and throughput KPIs for the float glass facilities are shown along with changeovers. The darker squares on the widget indicate a higher number and better performance. Above each of the widgets is the average for the entire corporation for each KPI.

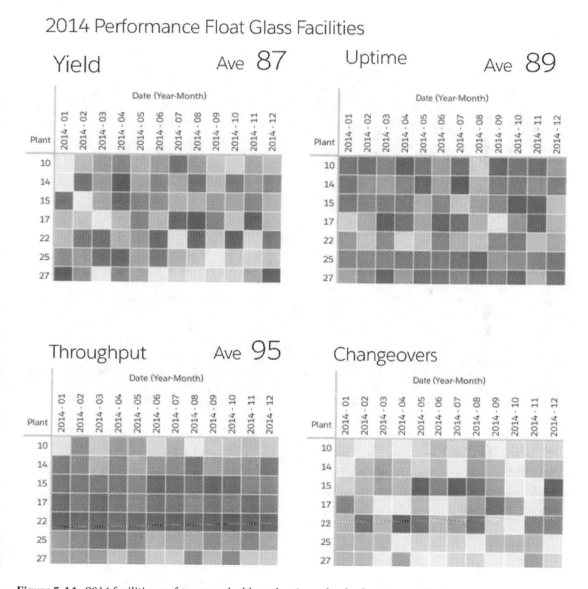

Figure 5-14. *2014 facilities performance dashboard, using calendar heat map widgets*

Simply by locating the cursor on any one of these squares, the user obtains the value for the relevant KPI on the heat map. The data shown is for year and month, the KPI, and the plant number. In Figure 5-15, the throughput KPI for Plant 22 is shown, for example.

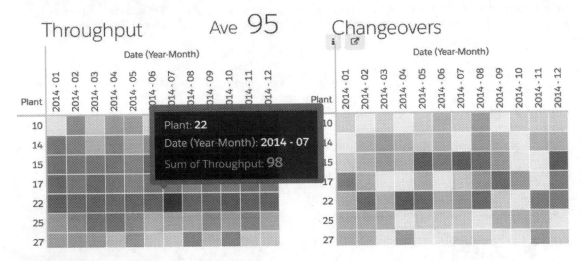

Figure 5-15. *Throughput data for July 2014, Plant 22*

A product changeover in a facility occurs when some aspect of the glass being produced is changed. These changeovers are tracked on the heat map in the lower right of the dashboard. Usually, changeovers involve alterations in glass thickness or color, and they often mean production downtime. It is a common belief that changeovers can be detrimental to a facility's production goals, yet some plants, like Plant 22, flourish despite a high number of changeovers. But how so?

In July 2014, there were five changeovers, consisting of glass thickness changes; however, the throughput and yield numbers were good, with throughput of 98 percent and yield of 93 percent. These positive results are easily seen in the dashboard—it's clear evidence that the plant manager at Plant 22 is performing at an exemplary level. Instead of fearing product changeovers, this plant manager issued a challenge to his team to find creative ways to manage the changeovers, and he provided incentives in the form of bonuses for reaching superior production numbers. The strategy paid off, and Plant 22 became an example for the rest of the corporation to emulate.

Traditionally, corporate management has relied on spreadsheets to analyze performance, but this approach does not come with the flexibility of the Salesforce Analytics Cloud, with its dashboards providing compact, comprehensive views that are updated dynamically, as well as the ability to refine the data. Figure 5-16 shows how managers could refine the data on this dashboard when they click one of the squares in the heat map.

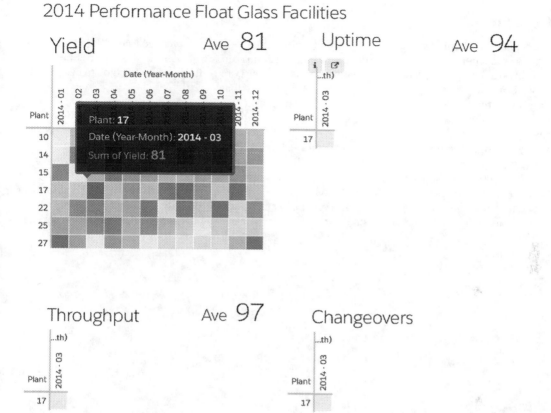

Figure 5-16. *Lower yield numbers for Plant 17 when March 2014 data is selected*

During this time, despite having uptime of 94 percent and throughput of 97 percent, the plant selected in Figure 5-16 was able to yield only 81 percent. Of course, these numbers are not always an indicator of poor management; sometimes a glass furnace is nearing the end of its life or needs a rebuild. The last rebuild of the glass furnace for Plant 17 was in 1994, so this is a strong possibility here. In any case, numbers like these are cause for concern and will initiate a deeper study by corporate management, but they were likely brought to attention because of the dashboard's readability.

Earlier in this chapter we discussed cognitive bias and how data-driven decision making can eliminate such cognitive bias. Assessment of plant performance and plant management is often susceptible to such cognitive bias. For example, a manager whose recent experience included working at a plant where changeovers consistently resulted in lower production numbers would tend to lean toward schedules that avoid changeovers so as to ensure production numbers are maintained. This is an example of recency bias. The downside to avoiding changeovers, of course, is a lack of flexibility in meeting market demands for product, leaving customers to find other suppliers. Looking at the high performance of Plant 22, one can conclude that changeovers can be managed, evidenced in the data.

Conclusion

As discussed in this chapter, cognitive bias can lead management to make illogical decisions based on incomplete or inaccurate data; these are decisions that satisfy an emotion need or fulfill a desire to be right. Everyone makes some wrong decisions or has incomplete or inaccurate information on which to base a decision; we are all subject to cognitive bias, without being aware that it exists.

The Salesforce Analytics Cloud, however, has the capability of nearly eliminating cognitive bias. We used the example of a glass company to show how presenting data in a quick and easy way can help managers to correctly diagnose the causes of equipment failures and production slowdowns. We contrasted the cases of two of the company's plants, with data revealing successful coping with changeovers for one and less satisfying production numbers for the other. The data in each case was presented in dashboards that offered easy access to additional details for evaluation and comparison.

We also saw how the Salesforce Analytics Cloud can be used higher up in an organization for personnel performance evaluation. This demonstrates the versatility of the Salesforce Analytics Cloud, especially its ability to perform in any situation and to enable users to be creative in making day-to-day decisions backed by solid data.

CHAPTER 6

■ ■ ■

Mobile Enterprise Data Discovery

A good plan today is better than a perfect plan tomorrow.

—General George Smith Patton

One of the most famous generals of World War II was George Patton, and the above quote is attributed to him. The statement reflects what Patton was best known for: taking action with the best possible information, instead of excessively analyzing situations. Patton was ardently opposed to digging in or establishing fixed fortifications, and he demanded of his troops constant forward movement. Given Patton's core values, he would certainly feel right at home with the mobile computing capabilities that are available to today's professionals through smartphones and tablet computers. Mobile devices allow these professionals to be productive away from their offices, as these devices no longer need to be tethered to a desk to be useful. In this chapter, we examine a moderate-size cycle company, the Ottawa County Bike Company, and how the Salesforce Analytics Cloud enables that company's personnel to use its existing decision support system data with their mobile devices to achieve greater insight into the company sales performance.

Data discovery enables key business stakeholders to use data in their decision making; this point has been emphasized in the preceding chapters and will be throughout this book. In today's business climate, staying on top of performance has never been easier with popular mobile devices and the Salesforce Analytics Cloud. Because of the "mobile first" approach of the Salesforce Analytics Cloud, users can access data discovery from their tablets, smartphones, and even from the Apple watch. Moreover, users can easily create their own applications, entirely via the mobile interface. In this chapter, all of the visualizations discussed are from the tablet or smartphone version of the Salesforce Analytics Cloud.

Overview of Our Use Case

Our use case for the Ottawa County Bike Company shows how a company that has followed a traditional approach to reporting can benefit from the Salesforce Analytics Cloud. The Ottawa County Bike Company has followed a disciplined, standard approach to enterprise computing since its founding some 15 years ago. The company has an enterprise resource planning (ERP) system to manage all aspects of the business, including basic business functions like human resources, payroll, and finance. The ERP system also has functionality that allows the company to manage sales operations, logistics, and channel management. Data from the ERP system is coalesced into a data warehouse. The data warehouse provides a comprehensive view of historic data, which is stored in indexed, de-normalized tables to facilitate rapid retrieval. Data tables in the data warehouse are the resource for many reports that the company uses for operational reporting. These reports were developed by business analysts using a reporting tool to arrange and format the reports.

The Traditional Approach to Reporting

The approach used by the Ottawa County Bike Company is one that has been used for many years to get reports into the hands of its business users and stakeholders. This venerable approach produces reliable reports through collaboration among business analysts, report writers, and stakeholders. The business analysts and report writers are part of a centralized report development team that resides in the information technology department. This department often has lengthy backlogs of requests for new reports or modifications to existing reports. Key decision makers can often get their requests fast-tracked, "cutting into the line" ahead of managers who may have been waiting for some time. Occasionally, to break up the logjam of report-generation requests, departments will hire their own report writers and analysts to address their needs. These dedicated report writers and analysts are sometimes the start of a "shadow IT" movement by these same departments, when those department continue to hire more IT resources such as developers, DBAs, and cloud app administrators. This fragmentation can be harmful in the long term, and can detract from overall corporate IT objectives of data standards, security, and architectural governance.

Often, companies that have already invested in many reporting or analytic tools are reluctant to consider any new investment in this area. Reporting and analytic tools have high annual support costs, ranging from 20 to 25 percent of the original costs of the product. Some companies have inadvertently acquired many reporting tools, either through mergers or because a tool was part of a bundled purchase of an ERP system or other enterprise software. It is not unusual for some of these tools to be abandoned when companies have many reporting tools, thereby squandering the original capital investment made in them.

An Alternative to the Traditional Approach

Figure 6-1 illustrates the traditional approach to reporting and analytics solutions, and shows how the Salesforce Analytics Cloud provides an alternative approach.

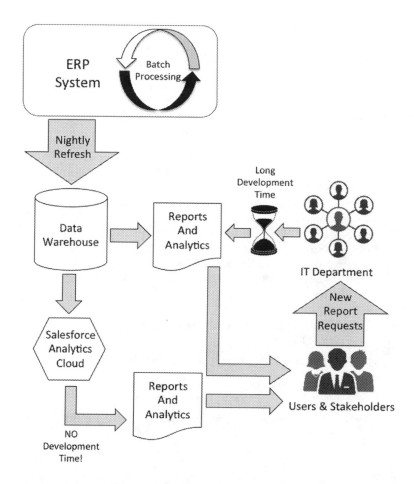

***Figure 6-1.** Traditional reporting approach with Salesforce Analytics Cloud as an alternative*

Even for companies with a painful past relationship with reporting and business intelligence tools, the decision to adopt the Salesforce Analytics Cloud is an easy one to make. The Salesforce Analytics Cloud is 100 percent subscription based, requiring no upfront capital investment. The subscription allows for individual licenses to be purchased in two categories, which makes it easy to keep costs under control, with the company paying only for the capability that is required.

Most business intelligence platforms require desktop computers for development and viewing of reports. Desktop computers are expensive to purchase and can be difficult to maintain. They also represent a security threat from viruses and malware, which is not a desirable situation when potentially sensitive data is involved. Additionally, report-viewing applications are often browser based, and they can have compatibility issues with different browsers, running on different versions of operating systems. This can result in high support costs and dissatisfied users when they cannot access their reports. With the mobile-first approach of the Salesforce Analytics Cloud, mobile devices like tablet computers and smartphones can be used to create reports and business intelligence applications. Mobile devices are inherently more secure than desktop computers because of the isolation of their operating systems from their applications. Mobile devices are well understood by nearly everyone from a usability standpoint, and the familiar gestures used on mobile devices are common to all applications, including the Salesforce Analytics Cloud. In general, the training required for mobile applications is on an order of magnitude less than desktop applications, and it can often be accomplished with online videos or tutorials. Tablet computers and smartphones also have the advantage of portability, especially for devices that have cellular network connectivity.

Perhaps the biggest advantage of the Salesforce Analytics Cloud is the ability to explore data. With the traditional reporting tools there is no capability to explore data, and alterations to any reports to reveal a new facet of data require that a request be made to business analysts or report developers. With the Salesforce Analytics Cloud, however, users are in complete control of their reporting and business intelligence experience, and they can drill into the data at will, as well as filter and organize the data.

The Use Case Architecture

While it is possible to integrate nearly any data source with the Salesforce Analytics Cloud using extract-transform-load (ETL) tools, a key feature of the Salesforce Analytics Cloud is its ability to get productive immediately, without complex and costly integration. In our example, the Ottawa County Bike Company IT department schedules an extract process from its data warehouse into a company Dropbox folder. The extract process writes a .csv (comma separated value) file to a Dropbox folder. Users with the Dropbox application on their mobile device can then access this .csv file and create their own applications.

▓ **Note**   Dropbox is a popular cloud-based file system that can be accessed from Macs, PCs, and mobile devices. There are even drivers for the major Linux distributions. Dropbox is one of several products in this class, including Google Drive and Microsoft OneDrive. Any of these applications is capable of serving files to the Salesforce Analytics Cloud.

The workflow for users at Ottawa County Bike Company to create their own applications is shown in Figure 6-2.

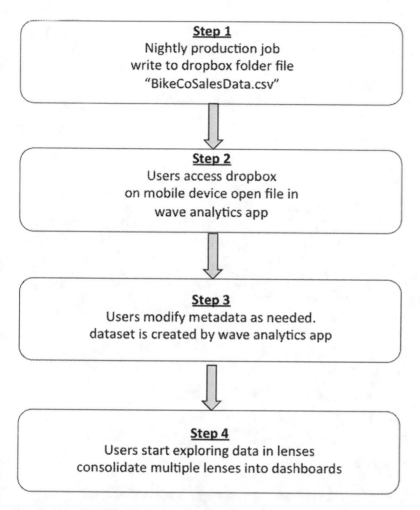

Figure 6-2. *Workflow for loading the use case data*

Let's take a closer look at each of these steps.

Step 1 – Output to .CSV File

This is the only step that is the domain of the IT department. Most IT departments typically maintain scheduling systems that run batch processes after hours. Scheduling systems provide the capability of running programs or processes associated with enterprise software in a set order, at a specific time. Scheduling systems also have the capability of running custom-developed processes. These can be processes developed on any platform, including extract-transform-load (ETL) software packages, or in a programming language like COBOL, Microsoft Visual Basic, Java, or Python. Figure 6-3 illustrates step one in this process.

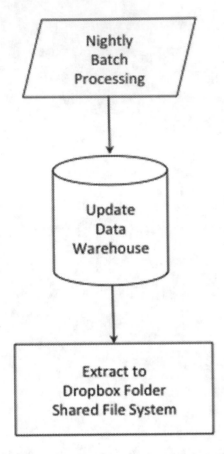

Figure 6-3. *Batch processing steps to produce extract file*

Batch processing involves the bulk processing of data for the ERP system and includes data from payroll, finance, and accounts receivable. When the batch processing is completed, reporting system databases, such as data warehouses, are updated with the latest data. The reporting system databases are updated and the reports are generated, so that users can view them the next business day. Also, extract files are created in common formats like .csv and JSON. In our example, this is when the file BikeCoSalesData.csv is created for our use case.

Step 2 – User Access of .CSV File on Dropbox

Step 2 involves users at the Ottawa County Bike Company accessing the Dropbox app on their mobile devices to extract the file BikeCoSalesData.csv. This is similar to the dataset creation that was shown in Chapter 2, but it differs in that here we are using the Dropbox iPad app as the starting point of dataset creation. On the Dropbox shared file system, there is a folder named "Extracts." In this folder is the BikeCoSalesData.csv file. Users select this file, then tap the "Open In..." button. This button lists all the apps that are capable of opening the BikeCoSalesData.csv data file. The list of apps appears above the "Open In..." button, and it includes a button for "Copy to Wave Analytics." Users then select this button to load the .csv file in the Salesforce Analytics Cloud iPad app.

The screenshots shown in Figures 6-4, 6-5, 6-6, and 6-7 show the series of steps involved.

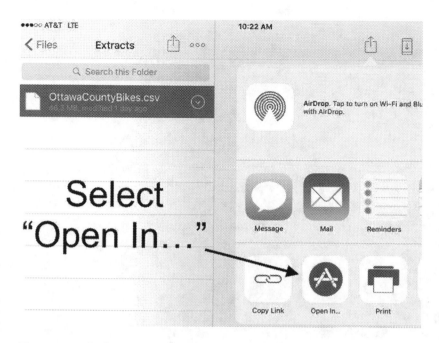

Figure 6-4. *The "Open In..." button*

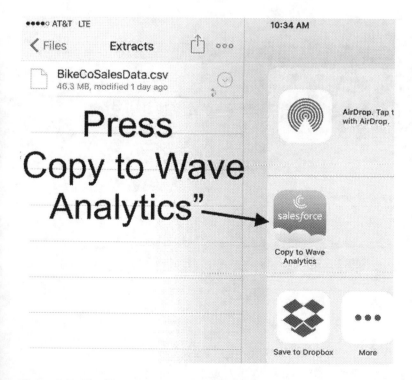

Figure 6-5. *The "Copy to Wave Analytics" button*

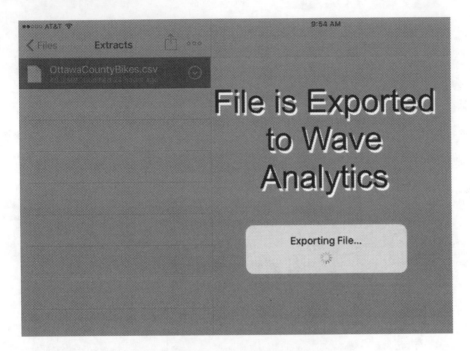

Figure 6-6. *The message indicating that the file is being exported*

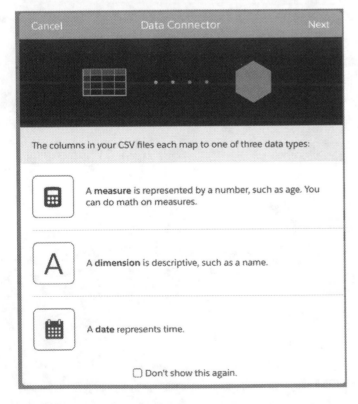

This first screen appears in Wave Analytics describing data types

Figure 6-7. *The first screen that appears in the Salesforce Analytics Cloud during file Load*

Step 3 – Modifying the Metadata and Creating the Dataset

Step 3 involves the actual creation of the dataset in the Salesforce Analytics Cloud. In Figure 6-7, there is a "Next" button on the upper right corner of the message box. Pressing this button reveals the metadata editor. From this editor, each of the columns in the OttawaCountyBikes.csv is mapped to one of three data types. Let's quickly cover these three data types:

- *Measures* are quantitative data, and within the Salesforce Analytics Cloud, users can analyze this data against one or more dimensions. Measures must be numeric data because within the Salesforce Analytics Cloud, mathematical operations are performed on the measures.

- *Dimensions* consist of descriptive data, and we evaluate measures against dimensions. For example, with a measure of total sales, one of the dimensions could be geographic region, such as state or province.

- Dates represent *time*, and they must be in a format that is recognized by the Salesforce Analytics Cloud as time data. Usually, data extracted from enterprise software databases is in the correct format. Often with this data type, only date information is present, with no time information.

Usually, the import process correctly determines the data types. However, in some cases, users may want to modify the data types. In the case of the data in the OttawaCountyBikes.csv file, there are quarterly numbers consisting of data that is entirely numeric. The import process assigns this to be a measure, but we actually want to use it as a dimension. When the import process finds a field that is purely numeric, it automatically makes the field a measure. Since quarterly numbers are attributes of data and add meaning to the measures in the data, they need to be changed to a dimension. Using the metadata editor shown in Figure 6-8, we can change "Calendar Quarter" to a measure simply by clicking the right arrow and selecting "Measure."

Figure 6-8. *The form to change data types*

It is sometimes prudent to review the number of decimal places to be used for measures. Noting this can make the data more readable, as in the case of "List Price" shown in Figure 6-9. We have selected two decimal places, since list prices are always expressed as an amount in dollars and cents.

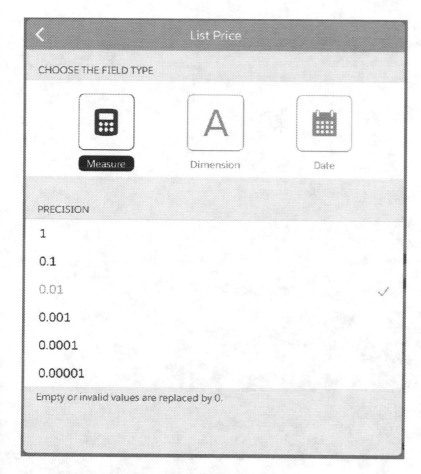

Figure 6-9. Changing the decimal places for a measure

One other interesting aspect of the field type selection is that it prevents users from making incorrect choices. For example, in Figure 6-10, we have tried to change "List Price" to a date type, but the import process has indicated that this action may not be correct.

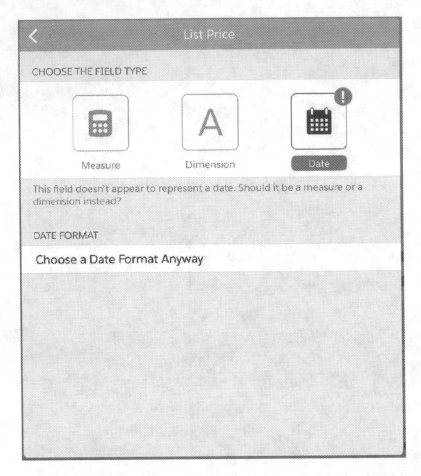

Figure 6-10. *Error shown for incorrect date field type selection*

The name of the dataset can also be modified on this message box. For example, the name of the .csv file is the default name for the dataset, but users are free to choose a different name.

Once we are satisfied that the data types are correct, we can start the import process by pressing the "Import" button in the upper right corner of the message box. As the dataset is imported, a message box appears indicating it is underway, followed by a message box indicating successful dataset creation. Small datasets are usually available immediately, but larger datasets may require up to an hour to be available.

Step 4 – Creating Lenses and Dashboards

Once the dataset has been created, users can immediately begin to explore the data, starting with the creation of a lens. This was covered in Chapter 2 of this book, so it will not be discussed here.

Data Used in Our Use Case

Now that we have covered the creation of the dataset, let's examine the data extracted for the Ottawa County Bike Company and how users can gain insight by using the Salesforce Analytics Cloud.

The data in this use case concerns sales performance. The Ottawa County Bike Company sells a wide range of bicycles, accessories, and components for bikes, as well as biking clothing. Its sales are through three types of entities: specialty bike shops, value-added resellers, and warehouses. Each row of data in the dataset tracks individual transactions and the sales function associated with those transactions. The columns in this dataset include the following that can be used in the Salesforce Analytics Cloud.

Sales Amount Data

Bank name: The financial institution handling the transaction.

Freight: The freight cost.

Discount amount: The discount given.

Total product cost: The total product cost.

Sales amount: The amount of the sale.

Tax amount: The amount for taxes associated with the sale.

Date Data

Order date: The date of the order of one or more products.

Calendar quarter: The year's quarter for the order date.

Calendar year: The year for the order data.

Product Data

Product name: The name of the product sold.

Product line: One of three values: mountain, road, or touring bike.

Product category: One of four values: bikes, components, accessories, or clothing.

Product subcategory: One of many values that more precisely identify a product. A few possible values include chains, brakes, caps, helmets, and mountain bikes.

Reseller Data

Full name: The sales representative in Ottawa County Bike Company responsible for the sale.

Reseller name: The name of the company originating the sale.

Reseller type: One of three values: specialty bike shops, value-added resellers, and warehouses.

Sales territory-country: The country of the sales territory.

Sales territory-region: The region within the sales territory country.

State/province name: The name of the state or province.

City: The city within the state or province.

Dashboard Development Cycle

Ottawa County Bike Company is a multinational company that makes and distributes products sold in U.S. markets, Canada, The United Kingdom, Germany, Australia, and France. North American is the biggest market for the company, and this business unit is the focus of the first dashboards we develop here. With the dataset created as described in the previous sections, we can now create lenses on the dataset that can be used to build dashboards.

To begin analysis of the sales data, we use the Sales Amount measure, and apply dimensions as needed to understand performance. To evaluate North American performance, we apply a filter to the Sales Territory—Country dimension, selecting United States and Canada. The dataset includes sales data for 2013, 2014, and 2015. The 2015 data has partial information for the third and fourth quarters, so the sales data for this year is incomplete, and this will likely be reflected in the dashboards.

For the primary chart on this dashboard, we select two time dimensions: Calendar Year and Calendar Quarter. The interface used to set the two filters on Sales Territory—Country and the two dimensions is shown in Figure 6-11.

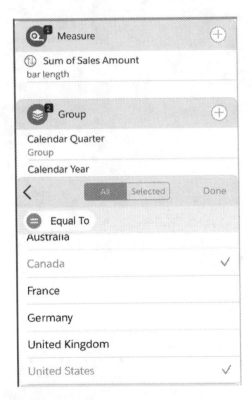

Figure 6-11. *Filter on Canada, United States, and group by measures of Calendar Year and Calendar Quarter*

Using these two dimensions with a horizontal bar chart, we develop an excellent visualization for quarterly performance. The initial version of the bar graph is shown in Figure 6-12.

Sum of Sales Amount
Groupings Applied Calendar Year, Calendar Quarter
Filters Applied Sales Territory Country in (Canada, United States)

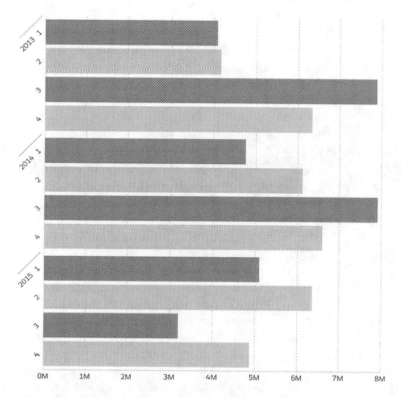

Figure 6-12. *Initial bar chart for quarterly performance*

The real power of the data discovery tools lies in their ability to apply refinements at will and display how the data changes. For this dashboard, we use the toggle widget to apply such refinements.

There are three refinements we use with the toggle widgets: Product Line, Sales Territory—Region, and Product Category. The dashboard with the widget in place is shown in Figure 6-13.

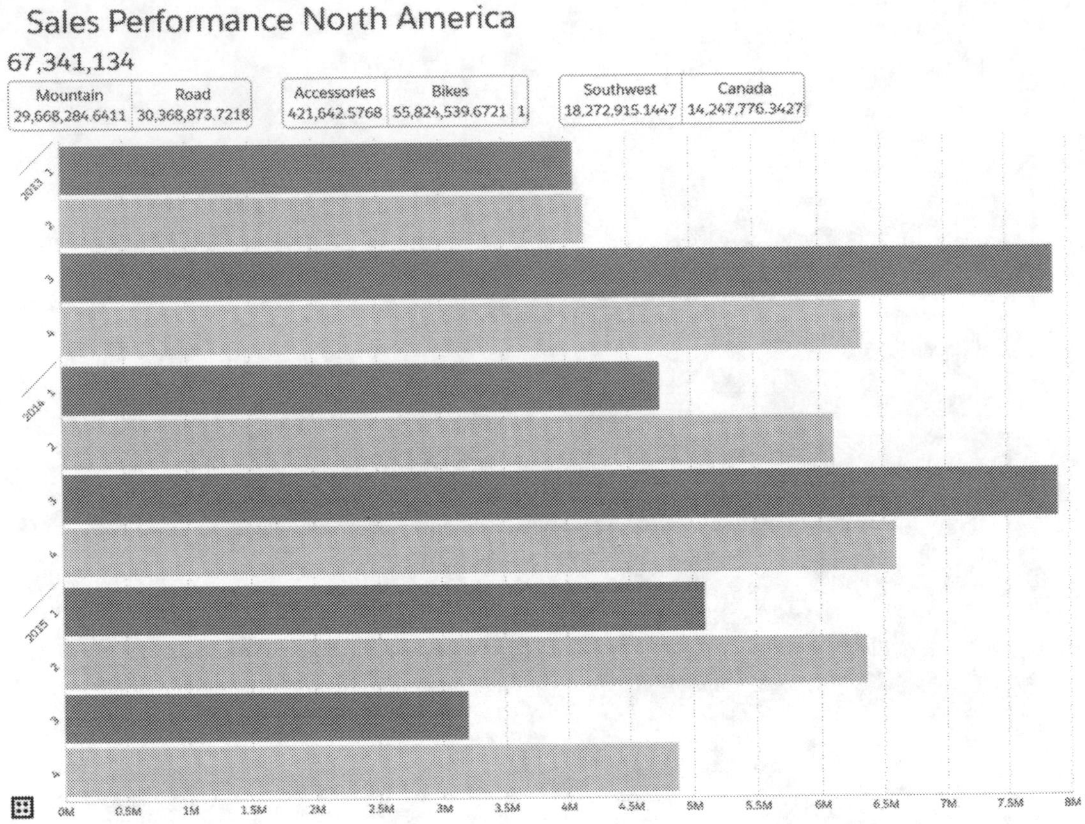

Sales Performance North America

67,341,134

Mountain	Road		Accessories	Bikes		Southwest	Canada
29,668,284 6411	30,368,873.7218		421,642.5768	55,824,539.6721 1,		18,272,915.1447	14,247,776.3427

Figure 6-13. *Sales Performance dashboard with widgets near top*

The widgets provide the ability to apply any refinement to the dashboard simply by pressing them. The widgets offer additional insight by indicating the relative contribution to the Sales Data measure for the dimension. For example, with no refinements applied using any of the widgets, and by simple inspection of the Sales Region widget, we can see that the Southwest region was the leading sales area, with $18,272,915 in sales, followed by Canada with $14,272,776. In similar fashion, the Product Lines selector widget shows that of the three product lines—Mountain, Road, and Touring—the Road product line is the clear leader, with approximately $30 million in sales, followed closely by Mountain, with approximately $29 million in sales. Note that on the mobile interface, the toggle control is "scrollable" by swiping either left or right to view other values. For example, if we scroll right on the Sales Region toggle, we will see other regions.

Let's get back to the bar chart for quarterly sales. With this chart, comparing performance from year to year for a particular quarter is easy. In the case of the first quarter, steady improvement is shown from 2013 through 2015, with sales of $4.1 million in 2013, $4.8 million in 2014, and $5.1 million in 2015.

To go inside the performance, though, we can click on a bar chart segment, and this quarter can be used as a refinement. For example, if we click on quarter 1 of the 2013 bar chart segment, we see the other widgets on the dashboard change to reflect the refinement. Clicking on quarter 1 or the 2014 segment changes the refinement—and again, the other widgets on the dashboard change to reflect this refinement. Figures 6-14 and 6-15 show this change.

Sales Performance North America
4,069,186

Mountain	Road		Accessories	Bikes	Clc		Southwest	Northwest	C
2,318,096.2865	1,751,089.7518		4,945.6925	3,877,493.2506	11,7(		1,010,044.894	859,414.4738	775,

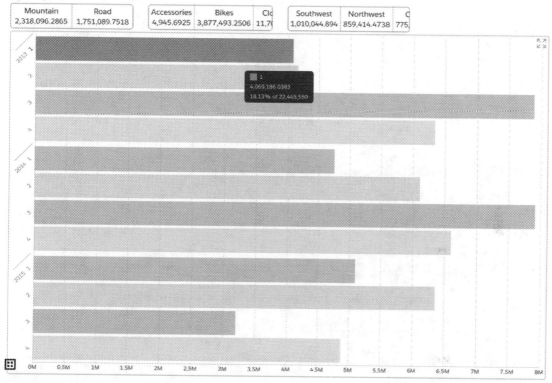

Figure 6-14. *Quarter 1 of 2013 is selected*

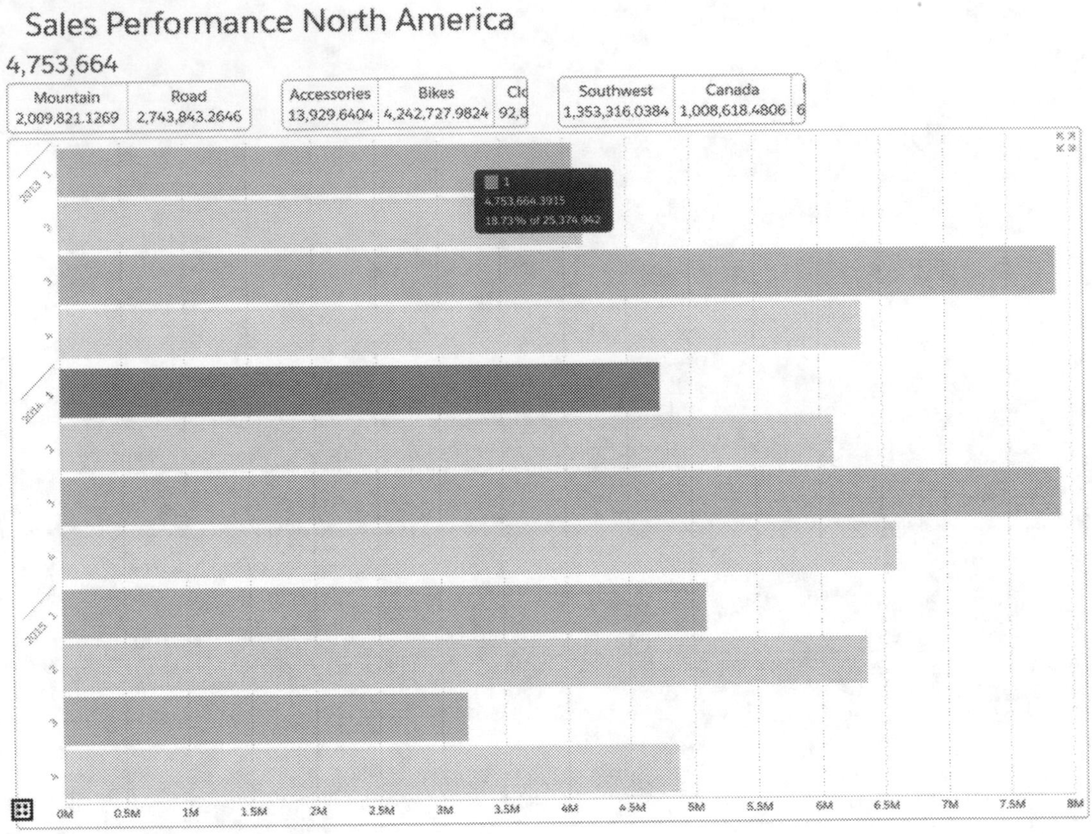

Figure 6-15. *Quarter 1 of 2014 is selected*

Digging Deeper

At this point, questions may arise just from using the dashboard. For instance, we established that first-quarter performance has steadily improved, but we have not learned the reason. Fortunately, with the Salesforce Analytics Cloud, we can quickly develop a new dashboard that allows us to answer this question! But before proceeding to develop a different dashboard, let's examine the question in more detail. Was the sales improvement due to increased performance for a particular region? For a particular product line? Or for a particular product category? As you will see, we can easily arrive at the answers to each of these questions.

To address this, we develop a dashboard with four bar charts. The first bar chart is quarter 1 for each year, which serves as a reference for the three other stacked bar charts. The stacked bar charts are for Sales Territory-Region, Product Line, and Product Category. This dashboard is titled "First Quarter Growth Study," and it is shown in Figure 6-16.

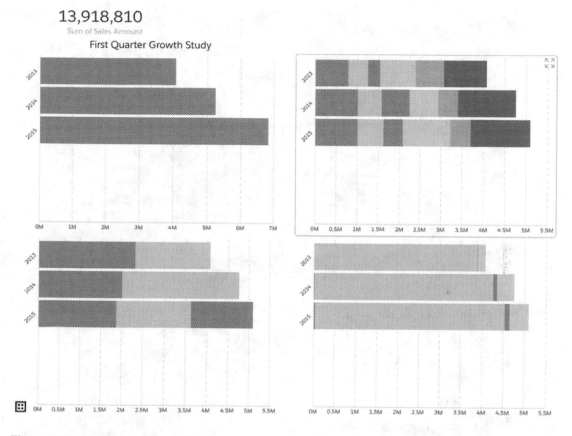

Figure 6-16. *First Quarter Growth Study*

The upper left bar chart shows the sales growth for the first quarters over a period of three years, and this is information we saw on the Sales Performance dashboard (Figure 6-15). The other three stacked bar charts have segments based on region in the upper right, product line in the lower left, and product category in the lower right. To examine each of these stacked bar charts, we press the icon in the upper right corner of the chart with four outward-directed arrows. The upper right bar chart, for Sales Territory- Region, is shown in Figure 6-17.

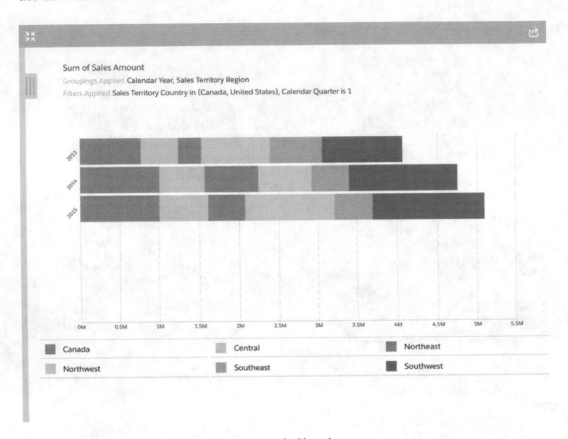

Figure 6-17. *Sales Territory-Region, Quarter 1, stacked bar chart*

From this bar chart it would appear that the Southwest region has seen steady growth over three years. It is easy to switch to another chart type, and sometimes there is an advantage to doing this. In this case, when we change to a line chart, the story behind the numbers is more obvious, with the line for the Southwest increasing steadily over the period—clearly the best performing region, as shown in Figure 6-18.

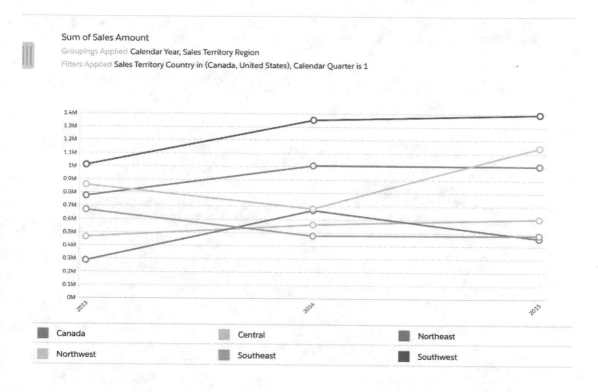

Figure 6-18. *Sales Territory-Region, Quarter 1, line chart*

For the other two bar charts, we also see interesting trends. Figure 6-19 shows the stacked bar chart for Product Line.

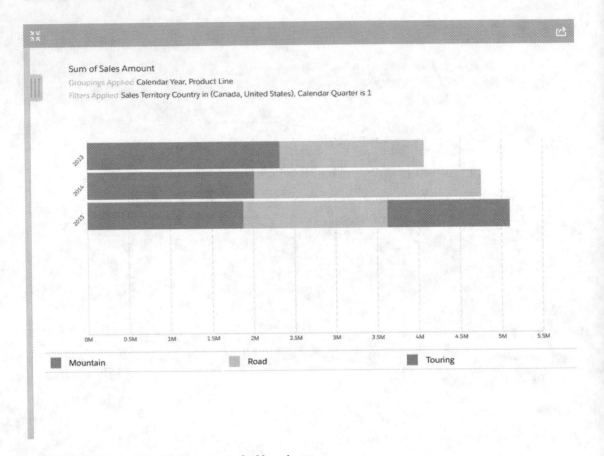

Sum of Sales Amount
Groupings Applied Calendar Year, Product Line
Filters Applied Sales Territory Country in (Canada, United States), Calendar Quarter is 1

Figure 6-19. *Product Line, Quarter 1, stacked bar chart*

In figure 6-19, we see that the mountain bike line experienced declining sales, and the road bike line experienced a surge in 2014, only to decline in 2015. The touring line, introduced in 2015, helped to maintain sales and offset the decline in mountain and road bike sales.

The last stacked bar chart is for Product Category, and is shown in Figure 6-20. The company saw growth in all areas, with bikes and components seeing the most growth.

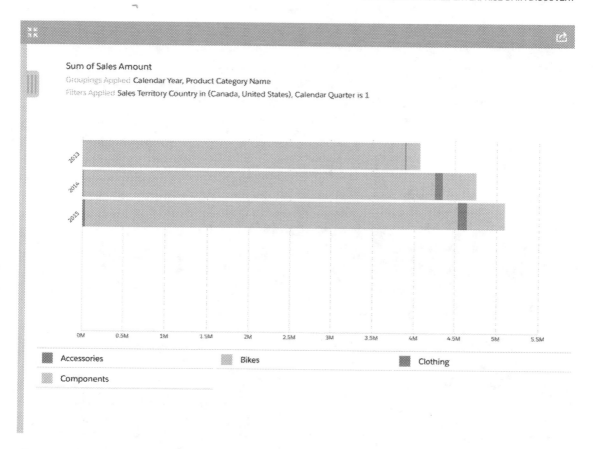

Figure 6-20. Product Line, Quarter 1, stacked bar chart

The four bar charts shown in Figure 6-16 were developed in a matter of minutes on an iPad, and they immediately revealed insights into the growth trends underlying the first quarter sales. From examining all the charts, we were able to conclude that the Southwestern United States was the strongest-performing region, and the introduction of the touring product line in 2015 helped to offset declines in the road bike line that had surged in 2014.

Since the theme of this chapter is mobile uses, let's look at how the First Quarter Growth Study appears on the iPhone 5S; it is shown in Figure 6-21.

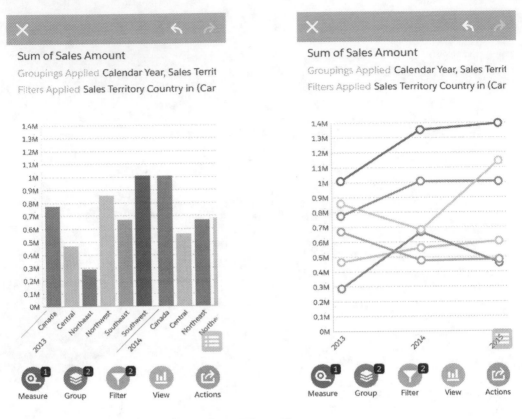

Figure 6-21. *First Quarter Growth Study, on iPhone 5S*

The iPhone's smaller screen requires scrolling, but it provides the same level of interaction as the iPad, allowing drilling into charts and modification of chart types.

To cover the full range of mobile devices, let's look at how the First Quarter Growth Study appears on the Apple Watch. As you would expect, the small screen provides a compressed view, but it is nevertheless understandable and the interface allows for drilling into data to view the actual numbers behind the charts. For those who sit through long meetings where smartphone use might be inappropriate, the Apple Watch allows an alternative way to access data discreetly. Figure 6-22 shows the First Quarter Growth Study on an Apple Watch.

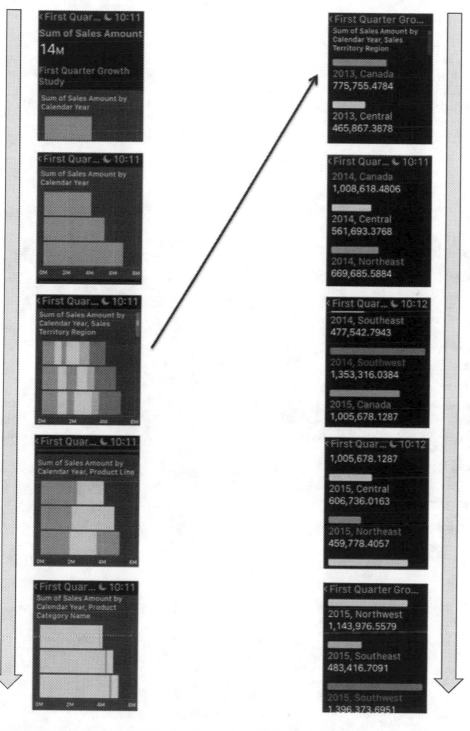

Figure 6-22. *First Quarter Growth Study, displayed on Apple Watch*

Adding Other Dimensions: Evaluating Individual Contributors

We can increase the utility of the sales performance dashboard by adding other measures. For instance, within each region, there are sales managers whose responsibility is maintaining and growing sales within their regions. Most users of the dashboard want to know the "players"—who are the best-performing sales managers. Adding this information to our dashboard is easily accomplished with a bar chart showing the names of the sales managers and their performance, as indicated by their contributions to the Sales Amount measure. Examining the bar chart with this measure, we can see that in North America, Nathaniel Grimes is the top sales manager, followed by Aki Hamanishi. This is shown in Figure 6-23.

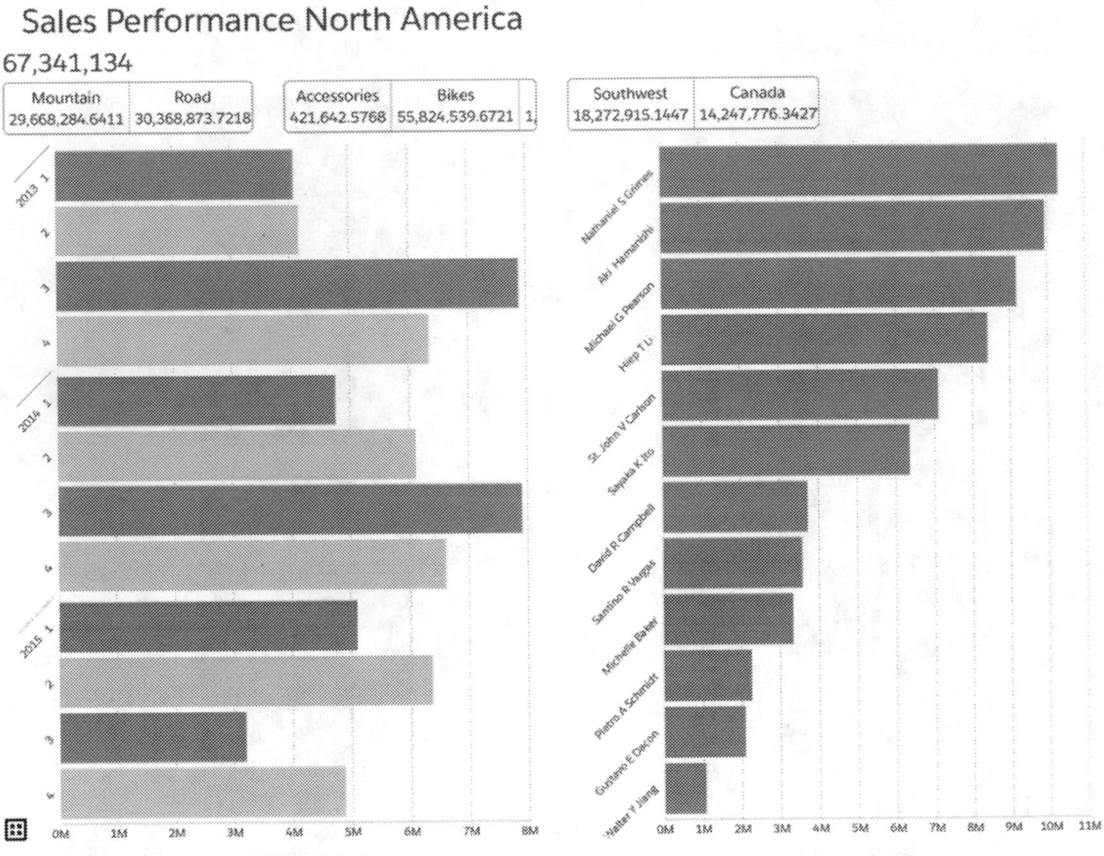

Figure 6-23. *Top sales managers*

By adding this bar chart to the Sales Performance dashboard, we can apply refinements, and thereby observe how sales manager performance changes. This is the advantage of the Salesforce Analytics Cloud: it allows us to dig deeper into data simply by adding new measures to a dashboard. As we apply refinements with the toggle widgets for Product Line and Sales Territory-Region, we can better understand the performance of the individual sales managers. If we select the top-performing Southwest region and the Mountain product line, we see that this is an area where Nathaniel Grimes performs best, as is evidenced in Figure 6-24.

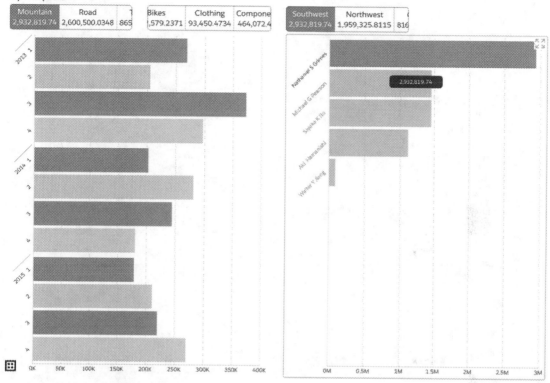

Figure 6-24. *Top sales manager for Mountain product line in Southwest region*

If we select the road line on the Product Line toggle widget, we see that Nathaniel Grimes does not dominate this area; instead, another sales manager, Sayaka Ito, is the top performer. This is shown in Figure 6-25.

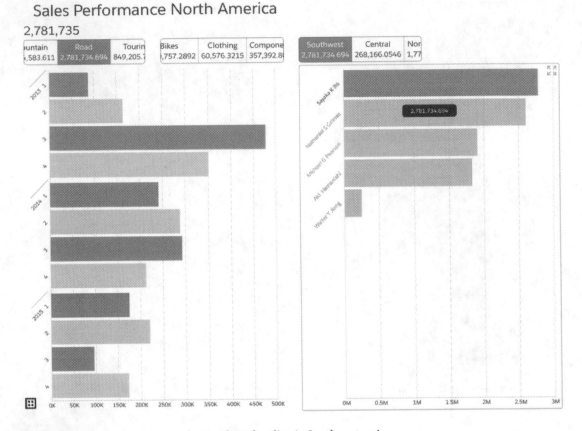

Figure 6-25. *Top sales manager for Road product line in Southwest region*

Analyzing Other Dimensions: Resellers

To demonstrate the versatility of the Salesforce Analytics Cloud, we will cover one last dashboard, with different dimensions and different data selectors.

The Ottawa County Bike Company uses three types of channels to sell and distribute its products, and this information is in the Reseller Type dimension. There are three possible types of resellers: specialty bike shops, value-added resellers, and warehouses. The dataset also includes information on the names of individual resellers in the Reseller Name dimension. Figure 6-26 shows a dashboard designed to analyze resellers, reseller types, and the top-selling products, which includes the sales managers, product types, and geographic regions. This dashboard is a good illustration of the versatility of the widgets in the Salesforce Analytics Cloud. For the product type and geographic region, a donut graph is used instead of a toggle.

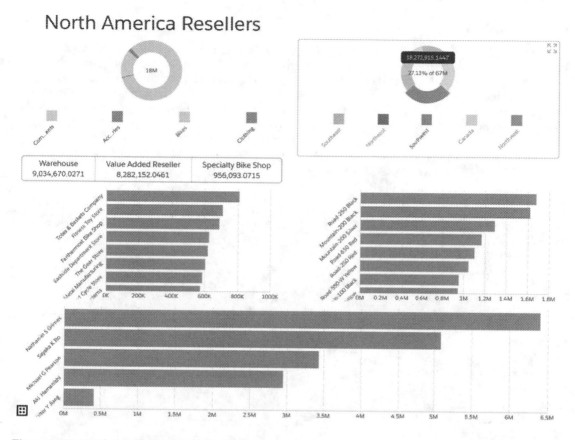

Figure 6-26. *North America Resellers dashboard*

In Figure 6-26, we have selected the Southwest region on the donut graph, and the other graphs have updated to reflect this selection. With this dashboard, it is easy to determine the top-selling products by geography, sales manager, or reseller type. This can assist with development of future sales strategies, because it can lead to an understanding of what products should be developed and promoted in particular markets.

Security and Shared Public File Services

Before we conclude this chapter, the topic of security and file-sharing services should be covered because it is integral to the architecture of the Salesforce Analytics Cloud. Earlier in this chapter, the popular cloud service Dropbox was used to make the .csv extract file available to Salesforce Analytics Cloud users in the Ottawa County Bike Company. While Dropbox provides password-based security, it does not offer any encryption of the files it stores. This makes it inappropriate for data that must be encrypted in accordance with regulation, such as is the case with HIPPA data. Dropbox is one of many possible file-sharing products that can be used for the Salesforce Analytics Cloud, and other file-sharing services should be evaluated for achieving an acceptable level of security.

Conclusion

The focus of this chapter was on the mobile capability of the Salesforce Analytics Cloud, and how it can be used to quickly develop dashboards that can be viewed on any mobile device, including the Apple iPad, iPhone, and even the Apple Watch. Using this mobile capability, users and stakeholders can develop their own reports and analytics solutions, bypassing the long development cycle of the traditional paradigm for producing reports. The use case showed how quickly and inexpensively this solution can be deployed. It also showed how new questions arise from the exploration of data presented via the Salesforce Analytics Cloud, and how these new questions can be quickly answered simply by developing new dashboards with new dimensions. The developers of the Salesforce Analytics Cloud have emphasized this mobile strategy, and this chapter demonstrates the benefits of this service.

CHAPTER 7

■ ■ ■

Advanced Data Acquisition and Processing

Know the smallest things and the biggest things. The shallowest things and the deepest things.

—Miyamoto Mushashi, *The Book of Five Rings*

Miyamoto Mushashi was a Japanese master of sword fighting who was undefeated after 60 matches. Mushashi's success was rooted in a deep philosophy of striving for complete knowledge of all things large and small. The same is true of information technology. Developing and maintaining an understanding of technical subjects across a broad range of areas means that you will have more knowledge and skills to attack problems when they appear and formulate innovative solutions to those problems.

With this philosophy in mind, we depart from a discussion focused strictly on the Salesforce Analytics Cloud in this chapter, and carry out a survey of some tools and technologies useful for acquiring data. This is followed by a discussion of data processing and the tools for data processing that make data available to analytics products like the Salesforce Analytics Cloud. The purpose of these tools is to make data available to analytics products like the Salesforce Analytics Cloud. The primary objective of this chapter is to raise awareness of these alternatives so that you can use them if the need arises.

The second half of the chapter introduces the Python language and presents two examples of its use in cleansing data for possible use in the Salesforce Analytics Cloud.

Data Acquisition—Tools and Technologies

There are three types of tools that deliver three different capabilities. We describe these tools in a general sense, without looking at specific vendor offerings, as there are too many to consider here.

Web Scrapers

Web scrapers are used to harvest information from websites. There are both commercial and open-source web scrapers available. Some commercial web scrapers have an additional capability of collecting information from documents like Microsoft Excel spreadsheets or .pdf forms.

Web scrapers use the document structure of web pages to extract specific items. Some advanced commercial web scrapers have a visual interface that allows scraping automations to be developed with little or no programming. These web scrapers can discover the document structure of web pages and show the fields as an overlay on the website.

Web scrapers are good for extracting information from websites whose structure does not change as the content changes. A common use of web scrapers is to extract reviews and comments on products from online retailers like Amazon. For example, a web scraper could extract all the opinion data for each product in an entire category, including customer comments and satisfaction ratings.

After web scrapers harvest the selected information, they save that information in a variety of formats, including .csv files. Many commercial web scrapers can write to relational databases.

Web Crawlers

Web crawlers programmatically collect information from a website. They can follow hyperlinks on web pages, navigating many levels into a website. They can be used to investigate a company's website, and are well suited to competitive research. Some commercial crawlers also offer the capability of crawling file systems and ftp servers to find office documents types like .pdf files, Word documents, and Excel spreadsheets, and then to extract information from them.

Web crawlers differ from web scrapers in that all text information is collected from a website instead of just specific items. Most web crawlers have depth settings that specify the extent of hyperlink navigation. A higher number set for the crawl depth means you collect more data—but it also requires more time to run. Web crawlers usually have a "politeness" setting that limits the rate at which requests are sent to the websites being crawled, so that the crawler does not overwhelm those web servers.

Crawlers tend to extract significant amounts of information from websites, so they can be difficult to manage without using other tools as well. Text analytics processors (described next) are commonly used to process the data acquired by web crawlers.

Text Analytics Processors

Text analytic processors are standalone applications that receive text from any source and locate specific entities in the text, like people, places, and things. They take the effort out of analyzing large amounts of text data. Many text analytic processors also provide sentiment analysis, or an overview of the positive, neutral, or negative status for a body of text. This feature is commonly applied when processing consumer comments on products. Text analytics processors can also summarize the output from both web scrapers and web crawlers.

Applications of These Tools

So, how are these tools applied to the acquisition of data? Let's examine a design pattern, with our example being some consumer research on data from a web retailer. The tools just described are used to extract data that can then be incorporated into the Salesforce Analytics Cloud, thereby showing overall ratings of the company's product, along with its price. This design pattern is shown in Figure 7-1.

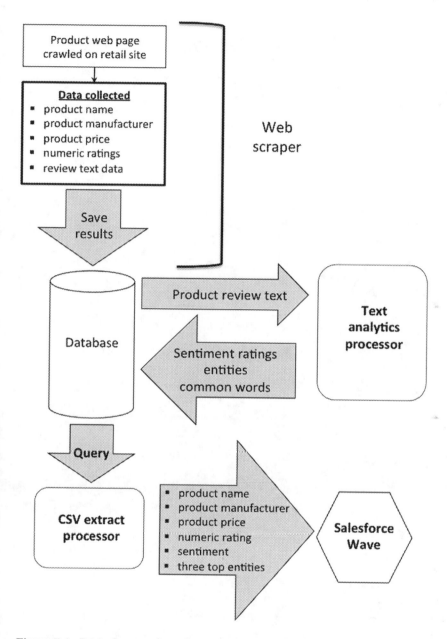

Figure 7-1. Design pattern for web scraper and text analytics processor

Although the Salesforce Analytics Cloud is oriented toward numeric data, it can still be used to analyze data from web scrapers. The web scraper extracts price and numeric ratings, which are numeric. The text analytics processor uses sentiment analysis to determine whether a product review is positive, neutral, or negative. The query consumed by the .csv extract processor contains one record for each review.

Figure 7-2 shows a dashboard that is created in the Salesforce Analytics Cloud with this customer review data.

BIKE PEDAL CUSTOMER REVIEWS

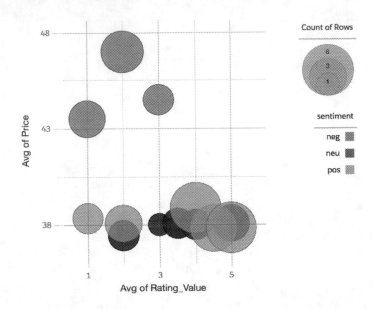

	Totals	
Average Rating	3.4	42
Positive Sentiment Rating	3.8	23
Neutral Sentiment Rating	3.7	10
Negative Sentiment Rating	1.9	9

#	⇕ Rating_Value	⇕ Rating	⬆ sentiment	⇕ Term 1	⇕ Term 2	⇕ Price
1	2	2	neg	Overpriced		45
2	2	2	neg			45
3	2	2	neg	Overpriced		48
4	1	1	neg	expensive	Overpriced	41
5	3	3	neg	expensive		43
6	1	1	neg	criminal		43
7	3	3	neg	company		45
8	1	1	neg	money		45
9	2	2	neg	dollar	bike	48

Figure 7-2. Dashboard created from customer review data

The dashboard provides a clear overview of the data. Customers who had paid more than $40 for the product left negative reviews. It is clear, however, that there is no correlation between sentiment and rating. Positive and neutral sentiments differ only by 0.1 in the average rating values. Ultimately, the raw data tells a story that confirms the correlations among negative sentiments, low ratings, and price, with terms extracted like "overpriced," "expensive," and even "criminal."

Note that rating and price were used as both dimension and measure in the dataset. This is because sometimes a numeric measure can often give insight about a different numeric measure when it is used as a dimension. In this case, price as both a dimension and a measure provides insight into rating.

Data Processing—Terms and Concepts

As mentioned at the start of this chapter, it is valuable to understand the nature of data processing and how a particular technology can be used. Simply put, data processing is the manipulation of data to make it useful. The Salesforce Analytics Cloud and other tools cannot use data unless there has already been data processing done on the data. As we know from Chapter 4, the Salesforce Analytics Cloud can only consume data that is in .csv format. But there is other data processing that must also occur to ensure that the lenses and dashboards in the Salesforce Analytics Cloud have meaningful and accurate data.

To better understand data processing, let's review some terms and concepts associated with it. These concepts include data wrangling, data standards, data quality and data cleansing, and enforcement of data standards.

Data Wrangling

Data wrangling refers to the conversion of data from one format to another so as to make the data usable. It often starts as a manual prototyping phase and leads to a well-defined sequence of steps. For example, Twitter makes data available about Tweets in a JSON document. If you want to put data originating in Twitter into the Salesforce Analytics Cloud, you need to extract the fields available within Twitter into a .csv file before it can be put into a dataset.

Data Standards

Data standards are rules regarding the format of data in an organization or held by governing agencies. Data standards ensure that the data in any system will be consistent with regard to formatting and content. Thus, data standards are usually enforced before the data is consumed and occurs when users enter the data or when the data is received from an outside source.

For example, many sources of data from suppliers or vendors use varying abbreviations for things like state names or road types. To ensure consistency, every occurrence of a road name in the address data might be changed to "Rd." and every occurrence of a street name is converted to "St."

Data Quality

Data quality is the extent to which data complies with data standards and is free of corrupt or incomplete records. Data that is fragmented and incomplete is considered low data quality and has a low level of compliance with data standards.

Data Cleansing

Data cleansing is the process of detecting and removing corrupt or incomplete records from data. Data cleansing may be performed in conjunction with data wrangling (see above). Data cleansing can also involve removal of duplicated records and enforcement of data standards. Data cleansing produces data with high data quality. Before data cleansing can be done on data, the data is usually called "dirty data." Dirty data is made "clean" by data cleansing.

Python: A Programming Language for Data Processing

Sit through enough conference presentations, and you will realize that not every task associated with data processing can be accomplished within the confines of the ETL tools discussed in Chapter 4, or with database server side programming or Java. Python has emerged as the golden thread stitching together many data-centric applications. It is the choice for many IT professionals, as it is a technology that can be used for data cleansing and wrangling.

At the 2015 Business Intelligence, Warehousing, and Analytics Summit, many thought leaders delivered presentations that involved Python being used to load or transform data. In the presentations at this conference, Python did not function in place of ETL tools, or database server-side programming, but instead provided the functionality or connectivity that is lacking in these other platforms. With so many popular programming languages like Java and Microsoft Visual Basic, why has Python become so popular for the tasks associated with data processing? When you look at the advantages of Python, it's not hard to understand.

Readability and Ease of Use

Many programming languages use special characters as delimiters for code blocks and statements. For example, in the "C" programming language, curly brackets ("{" and "}") are used to designate code blocks, and semicolons are used to designate the ends of lines. You can't get away from these special characters, even in the most basic "Hello, World" type program, like the one shown below:

```
{
    printf("Hello World");

}
```

It is a common practice for programmers to use indentation to organize their code. Python avoids the use of special characters and uses indentation to designate code blocks, since most programmers already use indentation to organize their code. In Python, the "Hello, World" example simply becomes the version shown below, free of special characters.

```
print "Hello, World!"
```

This readability makes Python easy to learn and use, especially by those who do not work as full-time programmers, but who need to perform data processing tasks—people like business analysts and database administrators.

Simplicity

Most programming languages expand and grow over time, and provide many different ways to accomplish programming tasks. A good example of this is the PERL programming language. The PERL programming language has been designed around a philosophy epitomized by the phrase "There is more than one way to do it," or TMTOWTDI. Python's philosophy rejects this approach. Instead, the Python approach is "There should be one—and preferably only one—obvious way to do it." This philosophy helps makes Python easier to learn and use than languages like PERL.

Portability

Python is installed by default on commonly used enterprise versions of the Linux operating systems, like Red Hat and SUSE. It comes installed on Mac OSX, and it can easily be installed on Microsoft Windows. It is also standard on Solaris, the Sun version of Unix, and can be easily installed on the IBM AIX UNIX. Because of this portability, Python code can be developed and prototyped on a workstation and then moved to an enterprise server.

Design and Debugging

Python features a command-line interpreter that allows easy testing and debugging of any command or series of commands. This eliminates the need for code to be developed entirely in editors. It allows simple programs to be tested line by line in the interpreter.

Versatility

There was a time when products that required batteries to operate would use the phrase "batteries included" to indicate the product was 100 percent ready to use, out of the box. Think of Python as the programming language that has "batteries included." There are feature-rich libraries that address any type of programming need, including data processing. We cover a few of these later in this chapter, but be assured that Python has libraries to connect to any data source and perform nearly any type of computation or data manipulation activity. A major reason for this is the strong user community that surrounds Python. This community includes open-source software developers, universities, and the private sector.

Python has broad acceptance among the best software developers. This is in part because of Python's adherence to proper computer science principles of computer language design. It has led Massachusetts Institute of Technology (MIT) to use Python in its course "Introduction to Computer Science and Programming." Additionally, many large organizations use Python extensively, including Google, NASA, and CERN. Python is a language used by highly skilled developers for massive, complex projects, while still being easy for more casual programmers to master.

Availability of Instructional Material

There are many instructional websites and videos for learning Python that are free and provide outstanding instruction. The aforementioned MIT course is available in online videos. Google also offers online Python instruction. If you consider using Python, check these out first.

Cost

Cost is often a reason organizations avoid ETL tools for data processing, as was mentioned before. Python costs nothing to license and use. Python's feature-rich libraries cost nothing to use, either. You can use any editor to develop Python code, including many free editors. There are good Python editors that provide more extensive syntax highlighting for less than $100 per user.

Two Examples Using Python

Let's examine two examples in which Python was used for data processing—or specifically, for data cleansing. Python is also well suited to other aspects of data processing like data wrangling, but we focus on data cleansing to keep the examples concise. Note: If you are not into code or coding, then you are likely to think these examples might not be for you. However, every reader should at least peruse these examples to get a sense for how much can be accomplished with very little Python code.

Data Cleansing Example 1

Chapter 6 featured the data for Ottawa County Bike Company. The data used was extracted from an ERP system for sales data. The data was contained in a .csv file that was loaded into Dropbox on an Apple iPad, and then subsequently loaded into the Salesforce Analytics Cloud. Having a duplicate record in this file would be a problem, because it would throw off all of the aggregations calculated on the dashboards. To eliminate this potential problem, a Python script is used to detect and remove duplicate rows. This script is shown in the following program listing. Figure 7-3 is a flowchart for this program.

```
1       #!/usr/bin/python

2       inputFile="/u01/import/csv/OttawaCountyBikes_dirty.csv"
3       outputFile="/u01/export/csv/OttawaCountyBikes.csv"

4       #  Clean up dirty ERP data
5       lines_read = set() # holds lines already "seen"

6       # Open output file for writing
7       outfile = open(outputFile, "w")

8       # Open file with dirty data for reading
9       for line_just_read in open(inputFile, "r"):
10
11          # Determine if line just read is NOT in lines_read set
12      if line_just_read not in lines_read:
13
14          # If line was NOT seen, write it to the output file
15              outfile.write(line_just_read)
16
17              # Add line just read to lines_seen set
18              lines_seen.add(line_just_read)
19
20      outfile.close()
```

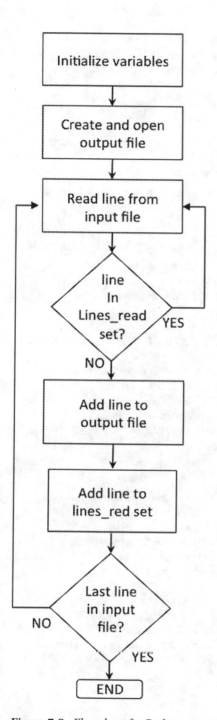

Figure 7-3. *Flowchart for Python example 1 data cleansing*

In example 1, there is a file with dirty data because the file could have duplicate rows. The data originated from the Ottawa County Bike Company ERP system, and the company has data standards that ensure data quality in the ERP, so we need only worry about duplicate records. In the program, the inputFile variable refers to the file OttawaCountyBikes_dirty.csv that contains data which has not been cleansed. The table below traces how this program works, line by line.

Line(s)	Comments
2	Variable "inputFile" is the name of the input file with dirty data.
3	Variable "outputFile" is the name of the output for cleansed data.
4	Declare a variable of type set(), "lines_read." The set type retains every line processed and is used to compare new lines.
7	Open output file for writing.
9	Open input file to read data to be cleansed, and loop through all lines in file, storing each line in variable "line."
12	Determine if the "line" just read is in the set "last_read." If the line is in "last_read," then it is a duplicate and will not be written to the output file. If it is NOT in "last_read," then write it to the outputfile because it is unique.
20	Close the output file, as processing is complete.

This relatively simple program takes advantage of Python's sophisticated data types, like "set" and its ability to perform comparisons with these types in a compact form. The variable declared as a "set" is "lines_read" and contains each of the rows that have been examined. The "set" data type includes a method ".add" that is used to add lines in our example. Without comments, this program contains only nine lines of executable code, and efficiently accomplishes the task of removing duplicate records.

Data Cleansing Example 2

In this example, we use data from the Ottawa County Bike Company that was also used in example 1. Recall from Chapter 6 that the Ottawa County Bike Company's products fall into four categories: bikes, bike components, clothing, and accessories. For two of these categories—clothing and accessories—the product distribution can include secondary distributors. Secondary distributors purchase the products from the warehouses, and then distribute them to resellers. Some of these resellers are online storefronts who can sell anywhere in the United States. Increasingly, this alternative channel has resulted in surging sales. However, information on products being sold online has been difficult to process.

A retail intelligence service provides a feed file that has information on product names and geographic information regarding the purchases that includes city, state, and zipcode. The online vendors often change product names inadvertently, and the city, state and zipcode information can be of varying format. To make sense of the data, we use an open-source library that performs fuzzy logic comparisons between the two datasets. The library is called Fuzzywuzzy, but before we use it, let's see how easy it is to install new libraries for Python.

Installing New Libraries

A compelling aspect of Python is the ease with which new libraries can be installed to perform a new function. In this example, we want to install the library Fuzzywuzzy, which performs fuzzy logic comparisons. To do this, we use the Python package manager "pip." Pip is a package manager that allows packages to be easily installed.

The syntax for installing new packages is simple:

```
$ pip install <package name>
```

Shown below is the command is used to install Fuzzywuzzy, followed by the output:

```
$ pip install fuzzywuzzy
Collecting fuzzywuzzy
  Downloading fuzzywuzzy-0.8.0.tar.gz
Installing collected packages: fuzzywuzzy
  Running setup.py install for fuzzywuzzy
Successfully installed fuzzywuzzy-0.8.0
```

This was executed on Red Hat Linux, but it also works on Mac OSX. Pip is not installed by default with Python, but installing it is easy—simply by running the following command:

```
sudo easy_install pip
```

Data Matching with Fuzzy Logic

Fuzzwuzzy compares two values and returns a percentage match. Let's see how it works, with a few commands executed through the Python command line.

We start Python and simply type the values shown, so as to experiment and prototype our use of the fuzzy logic match. We start by declaring two variables. The first variable, prodNameRef, contains the product name from the Ottawa County Bike Company database. The second variable, prodNameComp, contains the product name from the retail intelligence service mentioned earlier.

The Fuzzywuzzy library has a namespace called "fuzz" that is used to access all its methods. A namespace is the name used to reference a library in Python code.

There is a method called token_sort_ratio that we use to compare the two variables. In the first test, the two variables contain identical data and a value of 100 is returned, meaning the data in the two variables is a 100 percent match.

```
>>> prodNameRef="ML Road Frame-W - Yellow"
>>> prodNameComp="ML Road Frame-W - Yellow"
>>> fuzz.token_sort_ratio(prodNameRef, prodNameComp)
100
```

Another value from the retail intelligence service for product name is not as close to the value from the Ottawa County Bike Company database:

```
>>> prodNameRef="ML Road Frame-W - Yellow"
>>> prodNameComp ="Road Frame-W - Yel"
>>> fuzz.token_sort_ratio(prodNameRef,prodNameComp)
84
```

For this value, we have a value of 84, which indicates an 84 percent match. In the next test, there is no indication of color:

```
>>> prodNameRef="ML Road Frame-W - Yellow"
>>> prodNameComp ="Road Frame-W"
>>> fuzz.token_sort_ratio(prodNameRef,prodNameComp)
```

71

A 71 percent match is not a reliable match, since there are other colors like black and silver for these product descriptions. A match above 80 percent indicates a strong match. Armed with this knowledge, we can read each row of data from the retail intelligence service, and compare it to every value from the Ottawa County Bike Company database until a match is found.

Data Matching Program

To find matches in the retail intelligence service data, a .csv file with the correct names of products is compared to a .csv file with the product names from the retail intelligence service. The first ten lines of the .csv file with correct product names are shown below:

```
HL Mountain Frame - Black,Components
HL Mountain Frame - Silver,Components
ML Road Frame - Red,Components
LL Road Frame - Red,Components
LL Road Frame - Black,Components
HL Road Frame - Red,Components
LL Mountain Front Wheel,Components
ML Mountain Front Wheel,Components
LL Mountain Handlebars,Components
ML Mountain Handlebars,Components
```

The first ten lines of the file with the retail intelligence data are shown next:

```
Mountain Frame - Bl,Harrison Bike Company,Gibsonbug,OH,43431
HL Mountain Frame - Silver,Harrison Bike Company,Scottsdale,AZ,85252
ML Road Frme - R,Harrison Bike Company,Chicago,IL,60662
LL Road Frame - Red,Harrison Bike Company,Davenport,IA,52801
 Road Frame - Blk,Harrison Bike Company,Chenoa,IL,61726
HL Road Frame - Red,All Star Bicycle,Cincinnati,OH,45205
 Mountain Front ,All Star Bicycle,Durango,CO,81301
ML Mountain Front Wheel,All Star Bicycle,Catskill,NY,12414
Mountain Handbars,All Star Bicycle,Carey,NC,27511
ML Mountain Handbars,All Star Bicycle,Lake Tahoe,CA,96150
```

This is dirty data; it has product names that may not be correct. It also contains a city name, state abbreviation, and zipcode of where each item was sold. For this example, though, we are only cleansing the product names.

Notice that the dirty data has names that appear to be truncated or altered from the original, like "Mountain Frame – Bl," where "Bl" is usually black. Using fuzzy matching, we are able to pair records like this with the correct product name. The program below loops through the retail intelligence data and the reference data, and uses the `fuzz.token_sort_ratio` to perform a comparison between the two sets of data. The variable `strongMatch` is used to store the minimum match criteria, and is set to 80 percent.

This is a longer program than the last example, so we won't go through a line-by-line explanation. The output from the program is to the screen or console instead of to a file. This is so that we can check to see if the program is in fact finding good matches between the two datasets. Once this is verified, the program can be modified to write to a .csv file that can be used to create a dataset in the Salesforce Analytics Cloud.

```
1 #!/usr/bin/python
2 from fuzzywuzzy import fuzz
3 from fuzzywuzzy import process
```

```
4 inputFileRef="/u01/import/csv/listComponents.csv"
5 inputFileCompare="/u01/import/csv/compareProductsList.csv"
6 outputFile="/u01/output/OttawaCountyBikesProductsList.txt"

7 strongMatch = 80

8 # open scrape file and put in a list
9 fp = open(inputFileRef, 'Ur')
10 ref_data_list = []
11 for line in fp:
12     ref_data_list.append(line.strip().split(','))

13     # open
14     fp = open(inputFileCompare, 'Ur')
15     comp_data_list = []
16     for line in fp:
17             comp_data_list.append(line.strip().split(','))

18     outfile = open(outputFile, "w")

19     for l in ref_data_list:
20             a_list = str(l).split(",")
21             prodNameRef=a_list[0]
22             for line in comp_data_list:
23                     #print(line)
24                     comp_data_list = str(line).split(",")
25                     prodNameComp=comp_data_list[0]
26                     prodComp = fuzz.token_sort_ratio(prodNameRef,prodNameComp)
27                     if prodComp >= strongMatch:
28                             print "--------------------------------------------------"
29                             print "Ref    %s " % prodNameRef.strip('[')
30                             print "Comp   %s  " % prodNameComp.strip('[')
31                             print "Match %s " % prodComp
32 outfile.close()
```

The output from the program is shown next:

```
------------------------------------------------
Ref    'HL Mountain Frame - Black'
Comp   'Mountain Frame - Bl'
Match 85
------------------------------------------------
Ref    'HL Mountain Frame - Silver'
Comp   'HL Mountain Frame - Silver'
Match 100
------------------------------------------------
Ref    'ML Road Frame - Red'
Comp   'ML Road Frme - R'
Match 90
------------------------------------------------
```

```
Ref    'ML Road Frame - Red'
Comp   'LL Road Frame - Red'
Match 94
-----------------------------------------------
Ref    'ML Mountain Frame - Black'
Comp   'Mountain Frame - Bl'
Match 85
-----------------------------------------------
Ref    'HL Mountain Front Wheel'
Comp   'ML Mountain Front Wheel'
Match 96
-----------------------------------------------
Ref    'LL Mountain Frame - Black'
Comp   'Mountain Frame - Bl'
Match 85
-----------------------------------------------
Ref    'LL Mountain Frame - Silver'
Comp   'HL Mountain Frame - Silver'
Match 96
-----------------------------------------------
Ref    'ML Mountain Frame-W - Silver'
Comp   'HL Mountain Frame - Silver'
Match 92
```

This example shows the capabilities of Python for prototyping with a library like Fuzzywuzzy using the Python command line, followed by development of a program to validate the basic approach. Creating a dataset from the cleansed data into the Salesforce Analytics Cloud would then be the next step, by writing to a .csv file.

Python Resources

Python is already in widespread use by IT professionals because of its versatility and ease of use. If you're interested in learning more about Python, visit the website `http://www.learnpython.org,` which has free online tutorials where you can run Python code in a web browser. The instructional resources mentioned earlier in this chapter are also excellent for beginners.

One of the reasons Python is a great language for data processing is the rich set of code examples and libraries available on the Internet. If you are faced with a particular data processing task, you can easily find a Python code example or a Python library that meets your needs simply by using an Internet search engine. The best resource for finding Python libraries is the Python Package Index, or the PyPI. The PyPI is also referred to as the "Cheeseshop" among Python programmers. You can find the PyPI at the following URL: `https://pypi.python.org/pypi.`

The PyPI contains a listing of over 70,000 packages that is curated and broken into categories. There are over 2,000 libraries available for text processing. The PyPI also has a powerful search feature. In the second example, we used a library called Fuzzywuzzy to perform fuzzy logic data matching. Search for "fuzzy" on the PyPI, and you can find other Python libraries that are based on fuzzy logic.

Conclusion

This chapter examined three types of software tools that deliver three types of capabilities related to data acquisition. An example dashboard in the Salesforce Analytics Cloud was shown to highlight two of the software tools. We also discussed data processing and defined terms used to describe three data processing activities: data wrangling, data processing, and data standards enforcement.

The second half of the chapter was an introduction to the Python programming language, followed by two examples of data cleansing using Python. Equipped with the tools presented in this chapter, you can acquire data from web sources and file systems, and perform data processing on the data to bring it into the Salesforce Analytics Cloud.

Index

■ A, B

Aesthetic dashboards
  design principles, 55–56
  goals, 55
  steps to, 55
  usability, 55
  user problems, 55
Analytics Cloud Builder. *See* Dashboard design

■ C

Cloud Explorer, 15
  Apps, 36
    My Private App, 36
    playground data, 37
    Share button, 36
  compact list view, 18
  dashboards, 28
    development cycle, 32
    link back to lens, 34
    widgets (*see* Widgets)
    wrap-up, 36
  dataset, 17–19
  features, 17
  lense, 19
    comparsion tables, 26
    data exploration, 27
    dates, 22
    dimensions, 20
    graphic representation, 23
    measures, 19
    mobile lens, 28
    modifications, 27
  Salesforce console, 16
  Wave Analytics App, 16
  Wave Analytics platform, 16
  Wave lacks
    geospatial data, 38
    map, 38
    math functions, 38

    statistical function, 38
    text analysis, 38
    text processing, 38
Cognitive bias, 89
  overconfidence bias, 90
  recency bias, 90
  sunk cost bias, 90

■ D

Dashboard design, 39
  aesthetics (*see* Aesthetic dashboards)
  anatomy
    Dashboard State section, 70
    dynamic widget, 70
    JSON files, 71
    layout canvas, 71
    queries, 70
    types of, 70
  chart widgets, 52
  dashboard view, 53-54
  dataset loading
    Analytics Explorer homepage, 40–41
    metadata, 43
    Microsoft Excel, 39–40
    select menu, 41–42
    view dataset, 43
  designer view, 53
  dimensions, 52
  dimensions list, 44
  filters definition, 49–51
  grouping and replace tab, 47
  JSON definition, 72
  mobile dashboard designer
    dashboard creation, 64–69
    dataset, 56–61, 63
  SAQL script
    configuration window, 74
    Consumer Spending, 71
    designer, 71–72
    dynamic selection binding, 75

Dashboard design (*cont.*)
    JSON file and update, 74
    keywords, 71
    pigql statement, 74
    statement window, 73
  toggle widget, 46–47
  unique values, 45–46
  vertical charts, 51
  visualization type, 48
Dashboard development cycle, 124
  bar chart segment, 124–125
  contributors, 136
  digging deeper, 128
    first quarter growth study, 133–135
    sales territory-region, 129–131
    stacked bar chart, 132–133
  resellers data, 138
  sales performance, 126
  sales region toggle, 126
Data acquisition, 141
  customer review data, 143
  design pattern, 142
  text analytic processors, 142
  web crawlers, 142
  web scrapers, 141
Data cleansing
  flowchart, 149
  installation, 150
Data integration methods
  ETL tool, 77, 79, 82
    connectivity, 83
    data extraction, 84
    dataset, 84
    map source data, 84
  External Data API, 77–79
    csv format, 80
    dataset creation, 81
    JSON metadata file, 81
    restrictions, 81
    support documents, 82
    system job-process, 81
    upload files, 81
  Wave REST API, 79, 85
Data matching
  fuzzy logic, 151
  intelligence service, 152
Data processing, 145
  data cleansing, 146
  data quality, 145
  data standards, 145
  data wrangling, 145
  Phyton, 146
    data Cleansing (*see* Data cleansing)
    data matching (*see* Data matching)
    resources, 154

  cost, 148
  design and debugging, 147
  instructional websites, 147
  portability, 147
  readability, 146
  simplicity, 147
  versatility, 147
Datasets, 19
Data types
  decimal places, 121
  descriptive data, 119
  erors, 122
  forms, 120
  quantitative data, 119
  time data, 119
Design and Debugging, 147
Dropbox app, 116

▩ E, F

Enterprise resource planning (ERP), 111
Extract transform load (ETL) tool, 77, 82, 114, 115
  connectivity, 83
  data extraction, 84
  dataset, 84
  map source data, 84

▩ G, H, I, J

Glass company
  corporate-level report, 104
  facility level report, 96
    bubble chart, 103
    cognitive bias, 103
    daily production report, 99
    electrical data, 102
    maintenance technician, 100
    operators, 101
    production management team, 97
  manufacturing process, 90
    automatic control *vs.* computer
      technology, 92
    data networks, 92
    glass making, early, 91
    instruments, 92
    Statistical Process Control, 92
  plant manager performance, 106
  structure and facilities, 94
    encapsulation, 94
    fabrication facilities, 94
    float glass plants, 94
    organizational structure, 95
  throughput KPI, 96
  uptime KPI, 96
  yield KPI, 96

■ K, L

Key performance indicators (KPIs), 96

■ M, N, O

Manufacturing Execution Systems (MES), 92
Mobile dashboard designer
    dashboard creation
        bar chart widget, 67–68
        dashboard designer, 64
        donut chart, 69
        single number widgets, 66–67
        toggle Field, 65–66
        widgets, 64–65
    dataset
        dashboard designer, 63
        data connector popup, 59–60
        dropbox application, 56–57
        field type and attributes, 60–61
        file info view, 57–58
        import complete, 62
        upload file, 58–59

■ P, Q, R

Portability, 147

■ S, T

Salesforce Analytics Cloud, 9, 77
    architecture, 12
        ecosystem, 13
        mobiles, 12
    data discovery, 7
        data lake, 8
        data server, 8
        development and analytic interface, 8
        loading interface and APIs, 8
    data uncertainty, 5
    desktop platform, 10
    mobile platform, 9
    scarcity, 6

Security and file-sharing services, 139
Simplicity, 147

■ U

Use case model
    architecture
        dashboards, 122
        data types (*see* Data types)
        dropbox app, 116–118
        lenses, 122
        use case diagram, 115
    data discovery, 111
    date data, 123
    product data, 123
    reseller data, 123
    sales amount data, 123
    traditional approach
        alternatives, 112
        desktop computers, 113
        reporting, 112
User Interface (UI), 40

■ V

Versatility, 147

■ W, X, Y, Z

Widgets
    data display widgets, 29
        chart, 29
        compare table, 30
        number, 30
        raw data, 30
        toggle, 30
    display widgets, 31
        box, 32
        scope, 31
        text, 32
    selector widgets, 30
        data, 30
range, 31

Get the eBook for only $5!

Why limit yourself?

Now you can take the weightless companion with you wherever you go and access your content on your PC, phone, tablet, or reader.

Since you've purchased this print book, we're happy to offer you the eBook in all 3 formats for just $5.

Convenient and fully searchable, the PDF version enables you to easily find and copy code—or perform examples by quickly toggling between instructions and applications. The MOBI format is ideal for your Kindle, while the ePUB can be utilized on a variety of mobile devices.

To learn more, go to www.apress.com/companion or contact support@apress.com.